Pro-Life Pulpit

Pro-Life Pulpit

Preaching and the Challenge of Abortion

STEPHEN TU

WIPF & STOCK · Eugene, Oregon

PRO-LIFE PULPIT
Preaching and the Challenge of Abortion

Copyright © 2011 Stephen Tu. All rights reserved. Except for brief quotations in critical publications or reviews, no part of this book may be reproduced in any manner without prior written permission from the publisher. Write: Permissions, Wipf and Stock Publishers, 199 W. 8th Ave., Suite 3, Eugene, OR 97401.

Wipf & Stock
An Imprint of Wipf and Stock Publishers
199 W. 8th Ave., Suite 3
Eugene, OR 97401
www.wipfandstock.com

ISBN 13: 978-1-61097-357-1

Manufactured in the U.S.A.

Scripture quotations are from *The Holy Bible: English Standard Version*® (ESV®), copyright © 2001 by Crossway, a publishing ministry of Good News Publishers. Used by permission. All rights reserved.

Italics within Scripture quotations indicate emphasis added.

To Him

*in whom is life, through whom all things were made;
who came that God's fierce love might be displayed.
Conceived by the Spirit, He dwelt in a womb—
for nine months a woman was His walking home.
He knew not sin, and yet sin He became,
enduring the cross, despising its shame.
But He rose from the grave that we might be blessed,
receiving by faith His righteousness and rest.*

*And in remembrance
of every aborted
brother and sister,
son and daughter.*

"Breathe for me," they haunt my prayer
with infant dreams of drawing air.
I shrink from sharp and sudden fear.
I shrink because the knife is near.
I feel a light initial blow—
but to the death my dreams don't go.

If you could only hear and see
the interest group that lobbies me—
whose privacy is not a right,
whose lives will end before tonight—
how quickly you would mark the ruse:
a woman's right to plan and choose.

A century beyond our own
will marvel at the evil done:
the terror and the salt and blood
in clean suburban neighborhoods;
the killing of one child in five
while you and I were here, alive.

—Kathleen Pluth

Contents

Acknowledgments ix
Prologue xi

PART ONE: WHY PREACH AGAINST ABORTION

1. What's At Stake? 3
2. What Does the Bible Say? 17
3. What Has the Church Said? 31

PART TWO: WHO'S PREACHING, WHO'S LISTENING

4. Abortion and the Preacher 43
5. Abortion and the Congregation 61
6. Abortion and Pop Culture 71

PART THREE: HOW TO PREACH AGAINST ABORTION

7. Conception and Gestation 93
8. Labor and Delivery 104
9. Two Sermons 114

Epilogue 129
Appendix A Nursing and Feeding: Equipping the Church for Pro-Life Ministry 131
Appendix B For Further Reading: A Bibliographic Essay 134
Bibliography 145

Acknowledgments

THIS BOOK HAS ITS origins as a Doctor of Ministry thesis project completed under the supervision and mentorship of Jeff Arthurs at Gordon-Conwell Theological Seminary. Jeff saw, before I did, the good that this project might do for God's kingdom. I am indebted to him for his ongoing encouragement and guidance. If you find anything helpful in what I've written, he deserves much of the credit.

There are many others I need to thank, beginning with my beloved congregation, Trinity Pacific Church. They have heard me preach on abortion many times, and their questions, comments, and concerns are reflected throughout these pages. More than that, though, their generosity toward my family has been deeply affecting. It is a delight to be their pastor.

Scott Gibson read my original thesis and offered many helpful suggestions that I have incorporated where possible. This book is better for his input. Kathleen Pluth graciously gave me permission to use her poem "Breathe for me." It is at once chilling and poignant. I am glad to be able to share it with you. Clive Clarke, David Head, Myrtle Hume, and Mary Lou Robinson have been diligent co-laborers in the effort to end abortion. It has been a pleasure to work with them and others at the Richmond Right to Life Society. Susan Arnold, Lillian Buckley, Cheryl Fletcher, Terry Henry, Chris Kennedy, Keith Manry, Eric Nelson, Linda Passmore, Bill Smith, Russ St. John, and Tom Tokura have been great encouragers, and I am proud to have studied alongside such a faithful group of leaders. Several churches and Christian groups have heard me preach on abortion and have provided valuable feedback. I am grateful for their insights.

Many others have been so kind to me, both during my work on this book, and over the years. I would be remiss not to mention Stuart Appenheimer, Ben and Annie Bacola, Howard Fung, Hoby and Tonna

Lee, Toby and Loretta Mak, Lloyd Min, Sheena Nahm, Chris and Kristin Prabhakar, Phill Sohn, Ho-Ming and Katie Tsui, and Allen Ye. They are better friends than I deserve. I need to thank, in particular, Kumiko Nakagomi, who, while we were undergrads together at the University of Pennsylvania, showed me, with gentleness and conviction, the incompatibility of my Christian faith and then-pro-choice beliefs. She was the first person to tell me that abortion is a sin.

This book would not have been completed were it not for the lifelong, unwavering love and support of my mom and dad, the tireless cheerleading of my sister, Emily, and the seemingly limitless patience of my beautiful wife, Laura, who is the doting mother to our three precocious daughters, a pediatric resident, and all-around superhero. She is the very best woman I know. Our children, Samantha, Daphne, and Gillian, bring me immeasurable joy. Next to honoring Christ with my life, I desire nothing more than to make them proud of their daddy.

Finally, thank you to all the women and men who have shared with me their stories of grief, regret, and healing. It has been a humble privilege to journey with you in your pilgrimage toward wholeness in Christ. And to all the courageous pro-life preachers and workers, thank you for your sacrifice. I wish there was more I could do.

My prayer is that God would be pleased to use this book in such a way that it becomes no longer necessary; that my children will live to see a day when abortion is unthinkable and God's glory in all things is exalted by all people. *Soli deo gloria.*

Stephen Tu
Toronto, ON
Feast of the Annunciation 2011

Prologue

"A person's a person, no matter how small."

—Horton the Elephant

In Dr. Seuss's classic children's book *Horton Hears A Who*, an elephant named Horton accidentally stumbles upon a microscopic-sized race of creatures called Whos, living on a speck. Problem is, no one can see them. No one else, except Horton, can even hear them. Their lives are under constant threat, and Horton believes it to be his moral obligation to rescue them. He tries to convince others that there's life on this speck, but in vain. The kangaroos and monkeys think he's a fool. He's mocked, beaten, and worst of all, the very animals he's trying to persuade to help him save the Whos, want instead to destroy the speck in a pot of boiling oil. Horton is resilient though, and in the end he's able to get the Whos to shout in unison so that the other animals can hear their collective voices and finally see that Horton was right all along: there *is* life on the speck.

Horton is rightly read and understood as a "parable on ethics."[1] It speaks to the moral imagination. Much like the Whos needed an advocate, so, too, do the unborn.[2] A fundamental difference between the Whos and the unborn, however, is that the Whos could speak. It was their voices, however faint and soft, that together saved their lives. But

---

1. I'm indebted to Jennie McLaurin, a medical doctor and former Dean of Students at Regent College, for this term. For an appropriation of *Horton* in the field of medical ethics, see Jellinek et al., "Managed Health Care," 31–37. Readers interested in an anthropological analysis of *Horton* will find Boyd, "Origin of Stories," 197–214, to be informative reading.

2. I'm aware that some people aren't happy with what they perceive to be an out-of-context co-opting of this book by pro-life advocates. However, the theme of *Horton Hears A Who* is precisely that all human life is equally valuable, a theme both consistent with, and central to, the anti-abortion position.

the unborn are the weakest members of our society. They have no voice and cannot rescue themselves. They need us to intercede and act on their behalf. The urgency with which we must respond to abortion cannot be overstressed.

John Piper, pastor of Bethlehem Baptist Church in Minneapolis, has called abortion "the greatest evil in our culture."[3] He pleads with fellow pastors to "put their lives and ministries on the line in this issue," and laments, "The cowardice of some pastors when it comes to preaching against abortion appalls me. Many treat the dismemberment of unborn humans as an untouchable issue on par with partisan politics. Some have bought into the incredible notion that they can be *personally* pro-life but publicly pro-choice or noncommittal."[4] Piper's concern desperately needs to be caught by pastors throughout the world.

Despite the growing interest in preaching and social justice, reflected in a spate of books published over the last few decades, no full-length treatment on preaching and abortion currently exists. I hope this book will help to fill that sad and unacceptable gap. It's intended primarily for preachers of all stripes. If you're already convinced that abortion is a sin and have preached against it in the past, my hope is that you will be affirmed in what you've already been doing and find additional guidance on how to continue doing it well. If you're convinced that abortion is a sin but until now have avoided the subject from the pulpit, my hope is that this book will motivate you to begin addressing it in your sermons and give you some insight on how to do it. If you're unsure about whether abortion is a sin, my hope is that you will read this book prayerfully and that by the end of it you will be convinced to preach against it. And if you're a preacher who does not believe there is anything wrong with abortion, then I pray that you, too, might be persuaded to change your mind. For those of you who aren't pastors, who don't preach, don't put this book away just yet. I hope and believe there is valuable material here for you, too. Read it, then give it to your pastor and encourage him to preach against abortion.

I hope what you read in these pages will convince you of the need to preach against abortion and assist you in doing so in a biblically-faithful, factually-accurate, congregation-sensitive, and gospel-rooted way that helps your church understand the issue and engage in social action

3. Piper, "How is trying to stop abortion different?"
4. Piper, *Brothers*, 212; emphasis his.

against abortion. If we are to see abortion abolished in our lifetime, we must preach boldly.

My involvement with abortion has its origins in my ministry as the pastor of a local church and my role on the board of directors of a regional pro-life group.[5] Having talked with people on both sides of the abortion debate, spoken with pastors about whether or not they preach on abortion, and counseled numerous people—both Christians and non-Christians—who have had abortions, I came to the realization that many preachers either avoid the subject (for one reason or another[6]) or else vilify and condemn from the pulpit in such a way that their intonations do more harm than good.[7] The reality is too few preachers have understood their obligation to preach against the evils of abortion. As a result, too many people in our churches have failed to hear the truth about this matter. Perhaps a scene from my own pastoral experience will help.

Seth and Leah came into my office wanting to talk.[8] They had been married for three years, and to the rest of the world looked like they had everything going for them: successful careers and a healthy newborn daughter. But that morning they shared a secret with me that they had not told anyone else. Several years before they were married, while they were still dating, Leah became pregnant and they decided to terminate the pregnancy. Seth and Leah were both Christians when they had their abortion, but Seth told me, "I never heard a sermon about it before. None

---

5. There are some contemporary anti-abortion voices challenging the use of terms like "pro-life" and "pro-choice" as being overly individualistic, as though the mother alone is responsible for herself and her unborn child. Indeed, the notion that a mother has this autonomy over the developing baby in her womb runs contrary to biblical teaching—where the whole community of faith is called to be involved in the raising and nurture of children and the care and support of parents (particularly single mothers)—and social reality—where most often, women who choose to have an abortion feel as though they have no choice except to abort. In this latter instance, the term "pro-choice" can often be a misnomer. In a similar vein, the "pro-life" label can sometimes be misleading, as though abortion choice advocates are instead "anti-life" or "pro-death." I'm sympathetic to these concerns, however, I've chosen to retain the traditional terms due to the immediate impression one gets as to which side of the abortion debate is being referred to; that is, I've kept the language for the sake of simplicity. I also think it remains an accurate and helpful term. On occasion I will use the term "anti-abortion" as synonymous to "pro-life" and "abortion choice" as akin to "pro-choice."

6. Frank Pavone, national director of Priests for Life, suggests twenty-nine reasons why pastors avoid taking a pro-life stand. See his article, "29 reasons."

7. For examples of this latter group, see the documentary *Lake of Fire* (2008), directed by Tony Kaye.

8. Their names and some minor details have been changed.

of our pastors ever told us that abortion is a sin." Almost immediately after their abortion they both felt guilty and ashamed. "We realized what we did was wrong," Leah said, "but we were scared. We were scared so we had the abortion. And we were too scared and ashamed to tell anyone after." Seth began to sob. "I killed my own baby. A father is supposed to protect his kids and, instead, I killed my baby." This counseling session haunted me. Why, despite the fact I believed abortion to be a terrible sin, had I never preached on it? How, going forward, should I address the challenge of abortion? And how might other pastors respond, both to the Seths and Leahs in their congregations and to the issue as a whole?

One thing is certain: we must respond, and as pastors, we must respond (at the very least) from the pulpit. But the matter isn't so simple. Preaching on abortion must be, first of all, preaching. It must be rooted in Scripture and lead people to worship, or else it is nothing more than a lecture on ethics. In a 1999 *Leadership* article, Tim Keller, senior pastor of Redeemer Presbyterian Church in New York City, cautions preachers to ground their moral exhortations in the gospel. "Pushing moral behaviors before we lift up Christ," he argues, "is religion." He shares the following story:

> A woman who had been attending our church for several months came to see me. "Do you think abortion is wrong?" she asked. I said that I did. "I'm coming now to see that maybe there *is* something wrong with it," she replied, "now that I have become a Christian here and have started studying the faith in the classes."
>
> As we spoke, I discovered that she was an Ivy League graduate, a lawyer, a long-time Manhattan resident, and an active member of the ACLU. She volunteered that she had experienced three abortions.
>
> "I want you to know," she said, "that if I had seen *any* literature or reference to the 'pro-life' movement, I would not have stayed through the first service. But I did stay, and I found faith in Christ. If abortion is wrong, you should certainly speak out against it, but I'm glad about the *order* in which you do it."

Keller's concern is justified. Many people confuse the ethical obligations of Christianity for the hope of the gospel. They mistake implications of the gospel for the gospel, itself. "We, of all people," he says, "ought to understand and agree with fears about religion, for Jesus himself warned us to be wary of it, and not to mistake a call for moral virtue for the good news of God's salvation provided in Christ."⁹ I agree entirely with his emphasis on the priority of preaching Christ's work over, and in place of, our good works. Still, it is both possible and incumbent upon preachers to preach Christ and tell people about abortion in the same sermon. The two are not mutually exclusive. But how do we do this? This book is my attempt at an answer.¹⁰

Pro-Life Pulpit is divided into three parts that look at the why, who, and how of preaching and abortion. In part one we consider *why* preachers need to preach on abortion. We build a case for the necessity of addressing this issue from the pulpit by considering it from biological, socio-cultural, biblical, and historical vantage points. In part two we ask *who* our listeners are, while remembering our own charge as preachers. We consider both our responsibility as those entrusted with the gospel, as well as our need to understand our congregations. The final section of the book is concerned with *how* to preach against abortion and includes two of my abortion sermon manuscripts. Ultimately, my twin goals in this book are to convince you to preach against abortion and to offer some practical ideas on how to do it well.

Abortion is, to be sure, an issue that needs to be addressed from a number of angles. I have no delusions that preaching, on its own—that is, preaching that doesn't aim for, and result in, action—will change the way the world thinks about it. The public's views are shaped and affected by a variety of sources, and those of us concerned with seeing abortion abolished need to confront it in an appropriate manner. This means, for instance, we need both proactive and reactive strategies. We need better abstinence programs, as well as more crisis pregnancy centers. We need to be involved in the realms of law, science, entertainment, politics, and education. We need to remember the importance of post-abortive counseling and encourage our people to get involved. All of these are critical sectors of public life demanding intelligent engagement by those who believe abortion to be a sin; by those who know it is. But this book is

---

9. Keller, "Religion-less Spirituality," 26; emphases his.

10. For Christian leaders who think preaching on abortion distracts from the real business of gospel proclamation, one pro-life apologist says they "have it all wrong. Pro-life presentations, properly presented, don't drive people [away] from considering the gospel. Rather, they suggest to non-believers that maybe, just maybe, the Christian worldview has something relevant to say to the major questions of our day. And any worldview that can make sense of those questions is worth a second look" (Klusendorf, "My Challenge to Christian Leaders").

not about any of these areas, as important as they are. This book is about preaching, and is based on the conviction that biblical preaching is not only essential for social transformation, but is the primary catalyst for change. Our preaching ought to help equip the people of God for pro-life work. As theologian and ethicist Stanley Hauerwas observes, pastors "have opportunities to address moral issues that almost no one else in this society has—except for television. . . . At least preachers can enliven a discourse that is not alive anywhere else, and people are hungering to be led by people of courage."[11] May we be such people, and may our pulpits resound with the pro-life message of the gospel.

---

11. Hauerwas, "Abortion," 621–22.

PART ONE

Why Preach Against Abortion

1

What's At Stake?

A community which regards and treats its weak members as a hindrance, and even proceeds to their extermination, is on the verge of collapse. The killing of the weak for the sake of others hampered by their weakness can rest only on a misconception of the life which in its specific form, and therefore even in its weakness, is always given by God and should therefore be an object of respect to others.

—Karl Barth

During one of our regular meetings over coffee, John, a friend of mine who pastors a local church, told me he was feeling a burden to tell his congregation about the horrors of abortion. "I just don't know where to start," he confessed. "It's such a delicate and controversial subject. I don't want people to think I'm getting on some moral high horse and passing judgment. I don't want them to think this is nothing more than me on my soapbox. But at the same time . . ." His voice trailed off. "I don't know. It's just . . . I think abortion is wrong. I know it is. I think I need to do something about it. I want to. I know I need to preach on it. But I just don't know where to begin."

Where to begin. That's the subject of this chapter. If you're like my friend John, you may be feeling an increasing weight of conviction to preach against abortion, but are unsure of where to start. The best place to begin is by getting educated, and that starts with learning about the issue. The theme song to the old *G. I. Joe* cartoon series was right. Knowing *is* half the battle. And preaching against abortion is to enter into a battlefield of ideas and the emotions that come with them. We need to be well-equipped.

This means you need to have at least a rudimentary knowledge of embryology and fetal physiology.[1] Don't be concerned if you don't have a science degree. You don't need to be a doctor or a biologist to be able to read and understand the relevant medical literature. What's more, excellent resources written for lay audiences abound.[2] In addition to the scientific facts, you should also be familiar with the socio-cultural world of those who choose abortions. Who gets them and why? And finally, you'll need to be familiar with some of the most common pro-choice arguments and how to refute them.[3] As you begin preaching against abortion, the same questions and objections will come up again and again. You need to know how to address them.

Certainly, you don't need to be an expert in any of these areas. But you do need to be informed. Here are just a few reasons why:

1. The more you know about the issue, the more credible you'll be. Your congregation may look to you as the resident expert (or at least an informed thinker). They want to trust what you have to say.

2. Someone listening to you may challenge you after the sermon. You need to be ready to respond.

3. Learning about abortion will lead you to understand more about the women who have them, why they have them, and offer ideas on homiletic approaches you might, otherwise, not think of.

4. If you're going to empathize with your listeners, a good number of whom will have had at least one abortion, it's helpful to learn about what they went through and continue to endure, both physically and emotionally.

5. The better you understand the issue, the better you'll be able to love and serve your congregation and the unborn.

---

1. It's common in medical nomenclature to refer to unborn babies eight weeks and younger as embryos and those older than eight weeks as fetuses. For the sake of simplicity, whenever I refer to fetuses in this book, I include all unborn children, unless otherwise specified.

2. See Appendix B for a bibliographic essay describing some of these resources.

3. Certainly, the more you know about abortion, the better informed your preaching will be and the more confidence you'll have in what you're saying. Some other areas worth learning about include surgical and medical abortion procedures and current laws surrounding sexual and reproductive ethics.

There is a lot to know about abortion, and those of you just getting started may feel overwhelmed. Take heart. This chapter will help you get oriented.

EMBRYOLOGY AND FETAL PHYSIOLOGY

The argument that abortion should remain legal because biologists aren't sure when human life begins is bunk. Life begins at conception. Embryologists are in complete agreement about this. A survey of the leading textbooks bears this out. "The infant develops progressively from the single-cell fertilized egg to a highly complex multicellular organism," writes Susan Tucker Blackburn. "The genetic constitution of the individual is established at the time of fertilization."[4] Translation: life begins as a single-cell and, if not interfered with, develops in complexity into multicellular life. But there is no change in species. Our DNA is determined at conception. It doesn't change over time. Blackburn is hardly alone in her assessment. "Human development is a continuous process," say Keith Moore and T. V. N. Persaud, "that begins when an oocyte (ovum) from a female is fertilized by a sperm (or spermatozoon) from a male."[5] On the beginning of individual human life they say:

> Although it is customary to divide human development into *prenatal* (before birth) and *postnatal* (after birth) periods, birth is merely a dramatic event during development resulting in a change in environment. *Development does not stop at birth.* Important changes, in addition to growth, occur after birth (e.g., development of teeth and female breasts).[6]

Birth is certainly a milestone. We note it on birth certificates and celebrate it each year. But birth does not mark the beginning of human life. In case there's any doubt that this is what Moore and Persaud mean, they make their claim explicit: "A zygote [which results from the union of an oocyte and sperm] is the beginning of a new human being"[7] and "The intricate processes by which a baby develops from a single cell are miraculous."[8] Miraculous! Their point is not to be missed. Your life

---

4. Blackburn, *Maternal, Fetal, and Neonatal Physiology*, 79.
5. Moore and Persaud, *Developing Human*, 2.
6. Ibid.; emphasis theirs.
7. Ibid.
8. Ibid.

didn't begin eight weeks after you were conceived. Or six months after you were conceived. And it certainly didn't begin when you were born. You began as a single cell.

Human life—however small, however undeveloped—begins at conception. To say it doesn't is to be ignorant of the facts. Moreover, to acknowledge that life begins at conception but then to say that the still-developing life of the embryo or fetus is less valuable or significant than that of the pregnant woman is to misunderstand that development is a continual process. Yes, it's true that a fetus is less developed than a newborn infant. But the newborn is less developed than a toddler, who in turn is less developed than she will be as a teenager. Physical development, to say nothing of psychological and spiritual growth, continues long after birth. And this development commences once sperm fertilizes egg. Consider, for instance, that by day eighteen of conception the embryo's nervous system and cardiovascular system already begin to develop. By day twenty-four the digestive, skeletal, vascular, and genitourinary systems are forming. Arm and leg buds appear by day twenty-eight, by which time the respiratory system has also begun developing.[9]

This is why embryologists Ronan O'Rahilly and Fabiola Müller suggest, "The status of the early human embryo is an evaluation rather than a scientific question."[10] Those who disagree on abortion do so based on differences of belief over the value and worth of the unborn child and the role God plays in pregnancy, not whether or not the child is alive. Consider, for instance, the candid confession of a doctor in Nebraska who performs late-term abortions. He's honest about the evil that he does. "We do kill fetuses. It dies because we give an injection into the fetus that causes the heart to just slowdown."[11] *We do kill fetuses.* We kill them. They die. The science is indisputable: life begins at conception. The fetus is most definitely human. What is being debated in the public realm is how to define terms like "human being" and "person," and what value to ascribe to those who fit or don't fit the definitions. But as O'Rahilly and Müller note, this is not something science, alone, is able to determine. What's more, they're careful to suggest that the selection of any particular developmental milestone as the basis for determining

---

9. This data is adapted from the helpful charts in Blackburn, *Maternal, Fetal, and Neonatal Physiology*, 80–85.

10. O'Rahilly and Müller, *Human Embryology and Teratology*, 7.

11. Drash, "Abortionist and his No. 1 foe."

when a fetus is or isn't a "person" is, in a philosophical sense, "largely arbitrary."[12]

It's arbitrary because embryologists agree that the unborn child is living. This is why all definitions of abortion specify that it is the termination of a pregnancy before an embryo or fetus is viable; that is, before it is able to live *outside* the uterus. The clear implication is that it's already alive and living *inside* the uterus. But if the fetus is a living organism, what is it if not human life? We can play with semantics to the point where truth is obscured and unnecessarily complicated. We can define terms like "human being" and "person" in such a way that precisely those that need to be protected by our definitions are excluded. Ultimately, we must ask, Who gets to decide? Who makes the definitions? Lexicographers? Politicians? Lawmakers? Doctors?

Definitions can be plain wrong. During the slave trade, for instance, slaves weren't considered people and, therefore, weren't fully protected by the law. They were objects possessed by their owners. And objects don't have rights.

So what is a good definition? Few have better articulated what it means to be a person than the German Catholic philosophical anthropologist Robert Spaemann. Spaemann says, "Persons are not something *else* the world contains, over and above inanimate objects, plants, animals, and human beings. But human beings are connected to everything else the world contains at a deeper level than other things to each other."[13] We are not simply another animal species. We have far greater dignity and worth than cats and dogs. What's more, Spaemann says, "As human beings we are aware of another's gaze fixed on us. We are aware of the gaze of all others, the gaze of all possible others, the 'view from nowhere.'"[14]

The best we can do—indeed, what we must do—is acknowledge humanness and personhood. The unborn child at all stages of its development is a living human being and abortion kills it. Let's be crystal

12. O'Rahilly and Müller, *Human Embryology and Teratology*, 8.

13. Spaemann, *Persons*, 4; emphasis his.

14. Ibid., 15. Against those who argue that the fetus may be human life and may only eventually develop into a person, he argues, "There are, in fact, no potential persons. Persons possess capacities, i.e. potentialities, and so persons may develop. But nothing develops into a person. You don't become some-one from being some-thing" (245; emphasis his).

clear. Abortion is the murder of a helpless, defenseless person. We can't escape the fact that we have a responsibility toward the unborn.[15]

A SOCIO-CULTURAL LOOK AT ABORTION

Perhaps some statistics will paint an even clearer picture of what's at stake. In 2005, 1.2 million fetuses were aborted in the United States, and another one hundred thousand in Canada; or one hundred and fifty babies *in utero* each hour.[16] In the time it takes the average reader to finish this book, more than five thousand unborn children will have been legally killed on North American soil. The (pro-choice) Alan Guttmacher Institute estimates that more than forty-five million fetuses have been aborted since the landmark *Roe v. Wade* decision in 1973.[17] Today, more than one in five pregnancies ends in abortion[18] and one in three American women has an abortion by the time they turn forty-five. With numbers this stunning, it should come as no surprise that many of these women are in our churches. In fact, 43 percent of women who've had an abortion self-describe as Protestant and another 27 percent as Catholic. This is staggering and sobering.[19]

What more can we say about the millions of women choosing abortion? Why are they opting to abort rather than carry their babies to term and either raising them or giving them up for adoption? Let's try to answer these questions.

First, *what do we know about the women who are having abortions?* Some of the findings may surprise you:[20]

15. This is an extension of Oxford theologian Bernd Wannenwetsch's thesis in his lecture, "Angels with Broken Wings." While he doesn't refer specifically to abortion—his focus is on the severely disabled—he argues that we not only share a common humanity with those on the margins of society, but it's precisely those on the margins who have the most to teach us about our own humanity. Wannenwetsch recognizes that the marginalized live at the fringes of society, but urges us not to think of them as people who need somehow to be brought "in," "but, rather, [placed] at the center of any sound philosophy and theology of personhood."

16. U. S. Census Bureau, "2010 Statistical Abstract," and Statistics Canada, "Induced Abortion Statistics, 2005."

17. For a readable history of abortion in the United States, see Olasky, *Abortion Rites*.

18. Jones et al., "Abortion in the United States," 6–16.

19. These statistics may be found on the web site of the Alan Guttmacher Institute (www.guttmacher.org/).

20. The sources of the following statistics come from the Alan Guttmacher Institute

1. Half of the women who have abortions are over the age of twenty-five; half are under. Less than 20 percent are teenagers.
2. Five in six women who have abortions are unmarried.
3. Three in five already have children.
4. More than 35 percent of women who have abortions are Black, while only 14 percent of the general American population is Black.

What should we make of these figures?

First, while close to 20 percent of women who have abortions are teenagers, most aren't. In my conversations I've found that many people wrongly believe abortion to be essentially an issue affecting high school students. It does, but in reality, half of the abortions performed in the United States each year are on women over the age of twenty-five. One implication for preaching is that, at the very least, we shouldn't make the mistake of thinking only our youth groups need to hear this message. College students need to hear it. Single adults need to hear it. Women with teenaged children need to hear it. Childless couples who don't want children need to hear it.

Second, premarital sex is a major factor in the prevalence of abortion. Addressing abortion without addressing sex outside of marriage may, in one sense, be putting the cart before the horse. If people waited until they were married to have sex, the number of abortions in North America would be vastly reduced. As preachers, we must tell our churches of the beauty of sex within the context of an exclusive, committed, lifelong marriage, and the dangerous realities of sex outside that covenant bond.

Third, the majority of those women who've had abortions already have children, many with two or more. We should not think that because our congregations are filled primarily with couples that have kids, that they would not consider abortion. The statistics say otherwise.

Finally, why are Black babies so much more likely to be aborted than White ones?[21] A significant reason is the preponderance of abor-

---

and the Centers for Disease Control and Prevention (www.cdc.gov/reproductivehealth/Data_Stats/Abortion.htm).

21. Clenard Childress Jr., founder of BlackGenocide.org, says, "The most dangerous place for an African American to be is in the womb of their African American mother" (cited in Piper, "When Is Abortion Racism?" See, also, Craven, "Abortion, Poverty and Black Genocide," 231–43; and Pope, "Pondering Abortion." This issue generated

tion clinics in urban locations operated by organizations like Planned Parenthood. Consider the example offered by Susan Enouen, who relates some tragically disparate figures about abortion in Iowa: "the overall state percentage of African Americans is 2.1%. Des Moines itself is 8.1% black. Within a one-mile radius of the abortion facility, the percentage of African Americans is 26.5%."[22] Far from being an isolated case, this is, instead, representative of the abortion industry. Abortion clinics in the United States tend to be found in poorer urban locations, more densely populated by visible minorities.

This is certainly a complex picture, and we've only considered a small handful of figures, but they are enough, I hope, to give you an idea of the diversity that exists among women who have abortions.

Now let's consider *why women choose to have abortions*. There are a number of reasons:

The life-situation reason. This can take many forms, but consider as an illustrative example, a teenager who becomes pregnant after having sex with her boyfriend. If she decides to carry the baby to term and raise him, she may have to do it on her own. She'll miss time at school, if not drop out altogether. She'll find her job opportunities limited. If she already lives at or below the poverty level, there's a good chance that poverty will persist. Her present life-situation makes abortion look like a compelling option. Or take the case of a newlywed couple I spoke with recently. Both the husband and wife were in law school and weren't planning on having children for many years. But they became pregnant during their honeymoon and were considering abortion because they believed a baby would interfere with their education and life plans.

The emotional maturity reason. Many young women find themselves unexpectedly pregnant and don't believe they're ready to become parents. But emotional maturity goes beyond biological age. A woman may simply feel too irresponsible to become a mother, regardless of how old she is. Several women have said to me that they can barely take care of themselves and are in no place to care for a baby.

The financial reason. Financial hardship can make the prospect of raising a child—or another child, in the case of those who already have kids—downright frightening. Many women do want children, "just not

---

significant media attention in early 2010 with the launch of a controversial billboard campaign in Atlanta. See, for instance, Dewan, "To Court Blacks."

22. Enouen, "Planned Parenthood."

now." They want to have kids one day in the future when they perceive they will be more financially stable and secure, and better able to care and provide for their children. It is a tragic irony that many women choose abortion because they're concerned with the quality of a child's life.

The relationship reason. A significant number of women who have abortions do so at the behest of their boyfriends or husbands. Others don't tell their partners about their pregnancies for fear their relationship will end. A baby might jeopardize things. In both cases the importance of the romantic relationship outweighs the life of the woman's unborn child.

The "I'm done with kids" reason. Other women find themselves pregnant long after they thought they were finished with having children. I know of one couple that had three kids, all of whom had already graduated from high school, when they suddenly discovered they were expecting again. They had been looking forward to life as empty nesters and had already begun making travel plans when the wife took a home pregnancy test. The result was positive. This couple decided to keep the baby. Not all couples in similar situations do.

The genetic reason. Genetic testing and diagnosis of embryos can screen for chromosomal abnormalities months before the expected delivery date. When tests come back positive many women and couples opt to have abortions rather than bring a disabled child into the world. A recent medical study found, for instance, that over 90 percent of pregnancies in the United States where Down syndrome (trisomy 21) was diagnosed during prenatal screening ended in the baby being aborted.[23] Political philosopher Jean Bethke Elshtain describes the consequences of this twenty-first-century version of eugenics: "When we aim to eliminate one version of humanity—whether through euthanasia or systemic, selective abortion of 'flawed' fetuses—perhaps a suffering humanity but humanity nonetheless, we dangerously constrict the boundaries of the moral community."[24]

The gender reason. In parts of the world where male children are more highly valued than female ones, sex-selective abortion is a common practice. As immigrants from these countries continue to move to North American cities, the aborting of female fetuses in Canada and the United

---

23. Mansfield et al., "Termination rates," 808–12.
24. Elshtain, "A Cultural Disorder," 37.

States is becoming increasingly common. This new reality in some communities is reflected in an abnormal birth ratio of males to females.[25]

The "life is threatened" reason. On occasion the pregnant mother's life may be at risk if she carries the baby to term. Abortion may be the only option to save her life. Another increasingly common reason given for abortions involves couples who've used *in vitro* fertilization to become pregnant. They will often be confronted with the choice of multifetal reduction (also called selective abortion). If a woman is pregnant with quintuplets or sextuplets, for instance, doctors will often recommend aborting one or more of the fetuses to give the others a better chance of survival.[26]

The sexual assault reason. A very small percentage of abortions are done because the pregnant woman was a victim of rape or incest and can't bear the constant reminder of the evil done to her.

While this list isn't exhaustive, preaching that confronts the evil of abortion (and the pro-life work that will begin as a result of such preaching) will be more nuanced and balanced when we remember there are many (and sometimes overlapping) reasons women choose to have abortions. Our sermons and our counseling will be better for having thought this through.

RESPONDING TO ABORTION CHOICE ARGUMENTS

If you're going to preach against abortion, it's important that you have a handle on some of the most frequently voiced pro-choice protests.[27] Among the most common rebuttals I hear are variations of the following:[28]

---

25. The cover story of the March 6, 2010, issue of *The Economist* is titled "Gendercide: What happened to 100 million baby girls?" and describes this problem. For an example of sex-selective abortion on the rise in North America, see Mrozek, "Canada's missing daughters."

26. Recent medical technologies are moving away from implanting more than two or three embryos at a time. Nevertheless, many more are created and cryogenically preserved, though never implanted. This is another bioethical crisis that should be addressed by the church.

27. We don't have space to address all of their arguments here. You should consult one or more of the many terrific resources discussed in Appendix B for more help in this area.

28. I've addressed these and additional objections at www.prolifepulpit.com/.

1. "Abortion is sad, but it's better than bringing more unwanted babies into the world."
2. "It's not the place of politicians and governments, or anyone else, for that matter, to tell a woman what she can and can't do with her body."
3. "The fetus may be a human life, but the life of the mother and her freedom to choose what she wants to do is more important."

There are different ways to respond to these and other abortion choice protestations, but there are three biblical responses that I've found particularly helpful when it's Christians who raise the objections. First, the Apostle Paul says that "do[ing] evil that good may come" is slanderous (Rom 3:8). The motivation behind aborting fetuses that are unwanted may spring from a sincere and legitimate desire to improve the lives of existing children or the broader social fabric; but this is no reason to do evil. Second, to those who argue that a woman should have the right to do what she wants with her body, Paul reminds, "You are not your own, for you were bought with a price" (1 Cor 6:19b–20). It is not your body to do with as you please. Every part of our being, including our physical bodies, is to be used for the glory of God. And third, to those who argue that a woman's rights trump those of her unborn baby, I stress both parental responsibility and community obligation in child rearing. The idea that the decision to keep or abort a baby is an individual's decision is completely alien to Scripture, which repeatedly emphasizes the need to love one another (John 13:34–35; 15:12; 1 John 4:7).

These arguments from Scripture won't be nearly as effective with non-Christians as they are (or at least ought to be) with Christians. What approach do we take with those who don't put any stock in the authority of the Bible? One way to proceed is by asking probative questions. I do this sometimes by simply asking, "Who says?" Who says a mother's rights are more important than her fetus's? Who says governments can't tell women what to do with their bodies?[29] Who says abortion is better than bringing an unwanted baby into the world? What makes that person's or that group's opinion—and it is an opinion—the right one to hold?

---

29. The argument based on a fetus being a part of a woman's body is, in fact, scientifically untenable. The fetus resides in the woman's body but is not a part of her body the way her finger or liver is. The fetus has, and is, a body of its own.

If you proceed with this line of argumentation, you can, with practice and skill, get at the presuppositions that a person holds about the biggest life questions: who is God and who are we? And that, of course, is also a doorway into sharing Christ with them.[30]

Another tactic is to adopt pro-life apologist Scott Klusendorf's approach. His strategy is straightforward and involves just two steps: simplify the issue and make a case for life:[31]

First, simplify things:

> If you think a particular argument for elective abortion begs the question regarding the status of the unborn, here's how to clarify things: *Ask if this particular justification for abortion also works as a justification for killing toddlers.* If not, the argument assumes that the unborn are not fully human. . . . Until you clarify what's really at stake—namely, that we can't answer the question, can we kill the unborn? until we answer the question, what is the unborn?—there's no point advancing your case. . . . Most people on the street simply assume that the unborn are not human beings.[32]

Klusendorf calls this the "trot out the toddler" approach. Abortion debates are often made much more complicated than they need to be. If we consider how we would react to a particular question or situation by changing the scenario from an embryo or fetus to a toddler, we cut straight to the heart of the matter: is the unborn child a human being?

So, if someone raises the objection that the rights of the mother trump the rights of the fetus, you proceed by asking whether they'd say that the mother's rights outweigh her two-year-old's.

Once we've established exactly what's at stake in abortion, we move to present our case against it. Here, Klusendorf says, appeal to shared authorities like science and philosophy. Scientifically, we've already shown that the unborn, from the moment of conception, is a living human organism. Philosophically, Klusendorf argues that "differences of size, level of development, environment, and degree of dependency are not relevant in the way that abortion advocates need them to be."[33]

---

30. See Chang, *Engaging Unbelief*; Keller, *Reason for God*; Markos, *Apologetics for the 21st Century.*

31. See his brilliant book *Case for Life*. This is a worthwhile read for all Christians.

32. Ibid., 25, 27; emphasis his.

33. Ibid., *Case for Life*, 28. His approach is an adaptation of one first articulated by Schwarz, *Moral Question of Abortion.*

Size. Horton taught us, "A person's a person, no matter how small." My five-year-old, three-year-old, and six-month-old (not to mention my thirty-something wife) are smaller than I am, but no less valuable.

Level of development. Just as my children are smaller than I am, they're also less developed than I am. If level of development is what makes abortion permissible, then not only are embryos and fetuses less valuable than teens and adults, but infants and toddlers are also less valuable. Very few would argue that case.

Environment. "Where you are has no bearing on who you are," Klusendorf says.[34] If you move across the country you're no more or less valuable now that you're in Portland than when you were in Philadelphia. Your biological status doesn't vary depending on your geographic location. In a similar way, the unborn doesn't suddenly become a more valuable human when she's born.

Degree of dependency. Being dependent on another person doesn't make someone less human. If it did, those in need of routine blood transfusions, the post-autonomous elderly, and anyone who can't get by without the help and support of another would all be excluded from the human community. Simply because the unborn child is dependent on her mother doesn't make her less valuable.

When we make a case for life in this manner we show that the unborn are philosophically no less valuable than a toddler, teen, or adult. There may well be follow-up questions and objections that your listeners will have, but this is an excellent starting point with both non-Christians and Christians. You won't typically have much time to spend on this in a sermon, so simplify the issue and make a case, not only from the Bible, but from science and philosophy, that the unborn is no less valuable a member of the human community than any other human being.

CONCLUSION

Preaching against abortion means you need to know about abortion. While there is much more that can be learned than what I've sketched out briefly in this chapter, you don't need to be an expert, knowledgeable about every detail, before you're ready to preach. Consider, for example, when you preach on any given Sunday. You will never know everything there is to know. You can't be an expert in the biblical languages, philol-

---

34. Klusendorf, *Case for Life*, 28.

ogy, semiotics, Ancient Near Eastern culture, and every other area of learning that enriches biblical study and speech communication. And yet, you preach. You must. So it is with abortion. Learn what you can. Study hard. Be honest with your people. But when it's time to preach, preach. Don't worry about not knowing everything there is to know. Continue learning. Continue preaching.

2

What Does the Bible Say?

It's a beautiful day in this neighborhood,
A beautiful day for a neighbor . . .
Would you be mine? Could you be mine?
Won't you be my neighbor?
Won't you please, won't you please,
Please won't you be my neighbor?

—Fred Rogers

OUR CONCERN FOR THE life of the unborn is rooted in biblical teaching, although the Bible doesn't explicitly condemn abortion.[1] But this shouldn't come as a surprise. While abortion was a well-known practice in ancient times, it simply wouldn't have been a consideration for God's covenant people. Throughout Scripture, children are called a blessing. It's not surprising, then, that we don't find a command against abortion among the many other biblical prohibitions. As Old Testament scholar Meredith Kline has observed, "It was so unthinkable that an Israelite woman should desire an abortion that there was no need to mention the offense in this criminal code."[2]

Although Scripture doesn't specifically prohibit abortion, it's not uncommon to hear both pro-life and pro-choice advocates reference the Bible to advance their respective causes. Among the most commonly cited passages are Exodus 20:13 (par. Deut 5:17); Exodus 21:22–25; and

---

1. Old Testament commentator Ronald Youngblood says, however, the "unfeeling destruction of unborn fetuses [in the Bible] is sinful and calls forth divine judgment" (*Exodus*, 105). He cites Amos 1:13–14 and 2 Kings 15:16 as examples.

2. Kline, "*Lex Talionis*," 193.

Psalm 139:13–16. Some, like Richard Hays, suggest that appealing to any of these passages to argue either for or against abortion choice "make[s] only the most oblique contribution to our reflection on this issue."[3] I think this is only partly right. In fact, each of these texts can, and should, be used in preaching against abortion if they're understood rightly and wielded wisely.

EXODUS 20:13

Pro-life advocates will sometimes invoke the command against murder to persuade abortion choice proponents that what they're supporting is wrong (Exod 20:13; Deut 5:17). But as Hays points out, "No one in the debate is arguing in favor of murder. The issue is one of definition: is abortion murder or not?"[4] This doesn't mean that preachers should avoid this text as the basis for a sermon against abortion. It may legitimately be used for that purpose. And I think it should. But the preacher will need to take care to address the issue of definition that Hays rightly notes is central here. It's not enough to say, "Murder is wrong. Abortion is murder. Therefore abortion is wrong." Though that statement is true, a full treatment of this text within the context of preaching will need to unpack each of those three points. First, we need to show why the Bible calls murder a sin: it destroys a person made in God's image. Even here, we need to address important foundational questions. What does "murder" mean? What is "sin"? What does it mean to be made in God's image? Only after we've fleshed all of this out can we move on to the second point, that abortion is murder. And there we may need to appeal to the realms of science, law, and philosophy. Only then will our hearers be able to connect the dots for themselves and conclude with us that abortion is never the right choice.

EXODUS 21:22–25

While Exodus 20:13 can be used too quickly (though, nevertheless, rightly) by pro-life advocates to condemn abortion, Exodus 21:22–25 can be used too quickly (and, as I'll argue, wrongly) by pro-choice proponents to defend their position:

---

3. Hays, *Moral Vision*, 446.
4. Ibid.

When men strive together and hit a pregnant woman, so that her children come out, but there is no harm, the one who hit her shall surely be fined, as the woman's husband shall impose on him, and he shall pay as the judges determine. But if there is harm, then you shall pay life for life, eye for eye, tooth for tooth, hand for hand, foot for foot, burn for burn, wound for wound, stripe for stripe.

The passage presents two possible outcomes to the accidental striking of the pregnant woman. The exegetical difficulty lies in determining who—the mother, the child, or both—is understood to be harmed or unharmed in the struggle. There are at least three possible ways to interpret and understand this text, as the following table makes clear.[5]

	Case	
Interpretation	No Harm	Harm
1	Neither mom nor child is harmed	Either mom or child is harmed
2	Child dies, mom survives	Child dies, mom harmed
3	Child survives, mom dies	Child dies, mom survives

In the first interpretation the child is born *prematurely* and survives. If there is no additional harm to either the mother or baby resulting from the struggle, a fine is prescribed by the judge. If there is harm to either mother or child, the law of *talion* applies. In other words, if the child is born prematurely as a result of the brawl between the men, and subsequently dies, this becomes a capital offense. This is very much a pro-life passage when interpreted this way.

In the second interpretation the mother *miscarries* after being struck, leaving the unborn child dead. In this case, if the mother suffers no physical injury (beyond the miscarriage), a fine is applied. If, in addition to the death of the child, however, the mother is also physically harmed, the law of *talion* applies. Abortion choice advocates have jumped on this interpretation, claiming that the fetus has less value than the mother. If the

---

5. This table summarizes John Frame's discussion of this passage in *Doctrine of the Christian Life*, 717–32.

fetus were valued equally, they argue, the penalty for the one who causes the mother to miscarry would be capital punishment, since the law commands "life for life." But, as life isn't demanded in the case of "no harm," it seems to follow that we must not treat the fetus as a full-fledged member of the human race with the same rights as others.

What this argument fails to take into account, however, is the context in which vv. 22–25 are found. Just a few verses earlier the law code specifies that in cases of accidental manslaughter, capital punishment not be enacted even though a man has been killed (21:13–14). The "life for life" rule can't be stretched too far. If, in fact, there is an accidentally caused miscarriage in view in 21:22–25 (and not simply a premature birth), it's better to understand this in light of the punishment charged for accidental manslaughter.[6]

Moreover, because of the law regarding the accidental killing of another human being specified in Exodus 21:13–14, we should be surprised that the law of *talion* is prescribed in this interpretation in the case of harm to the mother. If the mother dies, life is demanded. But, one must ask, if her death was caused accidentally, why isn't the corresponding penalty simply a fine? John Frame says it's because "this passage gives a special protection to pregnant women and their unborn children."[7] In other words, this interpretation, too, far from being fodder for pro-choice proponents, has strong pro-life implications.

The third interpretation says a fine is charged if the mother is killed but the baby survives. If, instead, the child dies and the mother survives, the law of *talion* applies. In this reading, the harm or lack of harm done refers specifically to the unborn child. Again, we have a strongly pro-life stance, and in fact, regardless of which of these three interpretations you find has the most explanatory force, you're left with a pro-life explanation.

PSALM 139:13–16

A final text to consider is the prayer of the psalmist in Psalm 139:13–16:

> For you formed my inward parts;
>   you knitted me together in my mother's womb.
> I praise you, for I am fearfully and wonderfully made.

---

6. See Waltke, "Reflections," 3n3. The pro-life view endorsed by Waltke in this article is a reversal of his former position, which he describes in "Old Testament Texts," 99–105.

7. Frame, *Doctrine of the Christian Life*, 720.

> Wonderful are your works;
>> my soul knows it very well.
> My frame was not hidden from you,
> when I was being made in secret,
>> intricately woven in the depths of the earth.
> Your eyes saw my unformed substance;
> in your book were written, every one of them,
>> the days that were formed for me,
> when as yet there were none of them.

Hays says, "Of the passages adduced in the abortion debate, this one perhaps has the most pertinence. It portrays a symbolic world in which God is active in the formation of unborn human life in the womb, and God knows the individual even before birth."[8] But this psalm, he adds, is "a poetic affirmation of God's loving omniscience and foreknowledge" and "cannot be pressed as a way of making claims about the status of the fetus as a 'person.'"[9] While Hays's caution is an important one, I think he goes too far in stating "that its bearing on the abortion issue is very indirect indeed."[10] To the contrary, the very fact that the psalmist describes God as intimately concerned with the growth and development of the unborn child means it has very direct bearing on the abortion issue, though it addresses it indirectly. God's creative act is underway long before the baby is born. As one commentator puts it, "the mystery and wonder which is at the heart of human life [is] but a reflection of the mystery and wonder of God."[11]

Although the Bible doesn't mention abortion specifically, texts like Psalm 139:13–16 show us God's involvement in the life of the unborn. In this way, although a passage may not appear on the surface to have anything to do with abortion, scratch a little, dig a bit beneath the surface, and you will find that many biblical texts may be rightly and wisely used to challenge the prevailing views of abortion.[12]

---

8. Hays, *Moral Vision*, 447.

9. Ibid., 448. It must be observed, however, that just because the psalms are poetry doesn't mean they don't or can't teach theology. Poetic language, in its ability to express the otherwise inexpressible, is well suited to articulate profound theological truths. In fairness, this isn't a claim Hays makes, though it is one I've often heard. For an example of the study of theology in poetry, see Wannenwetsch, ed., *Who Am I?*

10. Hays, *Moral Vision*, 448.

11. Davidson, *Vitality of Worship*, 448.

12. I offer suggestions on how to do this in chapters 7 and 8.

SIN AND PERSONHOOD

One other important passage to consider is Psalm 51:5: "Behold, I was brought forth in iniquity, and in sin did by mother conceive me."[13] Notice the psalmist says that from the time he was conceived he was "in sin." As C. John Collins explains, "The idea is not that the act of conception was itself sinful, but . . . that each worshiper learns to trace his sinful tendencies to the very beginning of his existence—not only from birth but even from before that, to conception. (This certainly attributes moral accountability, the most important aspect of "personhood," to the developing baby in the womb.)"[14]

In other words, there is a clear continuity of our sinful nature from conception to adulthood. Sin, according to the psalmist, is imputed to each person when she's conceived, while she's still in the womb. "Potential" people aren't sinners, only people are. This has led Bruce Waltke to conclude, "The fetus is human and therefore to be accorded the same protection to life granted every other human being. Indeed, feticide is murder, an attack against a fellow man who owes his life to God, and a violation of the commandment, 'You shall not kill.'"[15] Far from portraying birth as the *commencement* of personhood, the Bible treats it as simply the *continuity* of personhood.[16] Personhood begins at conception. And the Bible is filled with instruction on how we are to treat other people.

THE PARABLE OF THE GOOD SAMARITAN

One such passage is the parable of the Good Samaritan (Luke 10:25–37).[17] You know this story well. An expert in the Old Testament law comes to Jesus to put him to the test. Like any test there's a question, and this test's question is: "What shall I do to inherit eternal life?" Rather than answer the lawyer directly, however, Jesus turns the question back on his questioner: "What is written in the Law? How do you read it?" In

---

13. Verse 7 in the (Hebrew) Masoretic Text; see, also, Judges 13:3–5.
14. *ESV Study Bible*, 1000 (note at Psalm 51:5).
15. Waltke, "Reflections," 13.
16. Luke 1:26–45 is another important passage that's been largely ignored in the church's thinking about abortion. See my sermon on this text, "The Incarnation of Christ," in chapter 9.
17. The discussion that follows is indebted to Timothy Keller's exposition of the parable in *Ministries of Mercy*.

other words, "You tell me," Jesus asks, "how do you inherit eternal life?" The lawyer gives it a moment's thought before replying, "Love the Lord your God with all your heart and with all your soul and with all your strength and with all your mind, and your neighbor as yourself." Give him credit because he's right. Jesus says so, himself. It sounds simple enough. If you want eternal life, love God and love your neighbor. Do this, and you will live. But the lawyer isn't through with his test. "And who is my neighbor?" he asks Jesus. "The implication in the question," says New Testament scholar Joseph Fitzmyer, "is, Where does one draw the line?"[18] The lawyer is trying to limit the scope of whom he has to love. If Jesus can more narrowly define who is and isn't a neighbor, it will make obeying the command (and inheriting eternal life) more easily obtainable. Once again, however, Jesus doesn't give the lawyer the answer he's looking and hoping for. Instead, he tells him a story.

There was a man journeying from Jerusalem to Jericho. This was a treacherous trip to make, and as it turns out, this man would not make it safely. He was assaulted by robbers and left for dead. Over the course of the day, both a priest and a Levite came upon the man, but both passed him by. Jesus doesn't tell us why they didn't attend to him, but we can make some reasonable, educated inferences. "While their behavior was certainly not commendable," Fred Craddock concedes, "neither was it without reason":

> The body on the roadside could have been a plant by robbers to trap a traveler. And certainly contact with a corpse would have defiled the priest and the Levite and disqualified them from their temple responsibilities. When they saw the victim, theirs was a choice between duty and duty. . . . Remember that this man who delayed his own journey, expended great energy, risked danger to himself, spent two days' wages with the assurance of more, and promised to follow up on his activity was ceremonially unclean, socially an outcast, and religiously a heretic.[19]

It's worth belaboring this point a little bit. George Caird says, "It is essential to the point of the story that the traveller was left half-dead. The priest and the Levite could not tell without touching him whether he was dead or alive; and it weighed more with them that he might be dead and defiling to the touch of those whose business was with holy things than

18. Fitzmyer, *Gospel according to Luke*, 886n10.
19. Craddock, *Luke*, 151.

that he might be alive and in need of care."[20] In other words, the man might have been dead, and yes, by the letter of the Old Testament law, the priest and the Levite would have become ceremonially unclean by touching him (Lev 21:1–3; Num 5:2; 19:2–13). But the man might have been alive—indeed he was—and yet they did nothing.

A little while later a Samaritan came across the man. Remember that Samaritans and Jews were bitter enemies (Luke 9:52–53; John 4:9). The Samaritan had no reason to stop and every reason to do like the priest and Levite and continue on his journey. Unlike the two religious professionals who preceded him, however, the Samaritan didn't merely go about his own way. "When he saw him," Jesus says, "he had compassion." The priest and the Levite may also have had compassionate feelings. Jesus doesn't tell us, and we shouldn't press where the text is silent. For all we know, they may have felt bad for the man's condition. They may have felt sorry for him and, perhaps, even prayed for him as they passed by. Certainly, they wouldn't have assaulted the man like the robbers had. In other words, they were both pro-life, at least at the level of belief. They may really have wanted to help him. We don't know. But we do know that the Samaritan had more than feelings. His compassion took the form of costly action. Stopping on his journey without knowing whether or not the bandits who attacked the wounded man were still lurking in the shadows was risk enough. But the Samaritan bandaged him, nursed him with the medicines he had, and took him to an inn for further care and treatment. He paid for the man's lodging and promised to pay the innkeeper whatever additional cost might be involved in attending to him.

After telling this story, Jesus turns back to the lawyer and asks him, "Who was a neighbor to the man who fell among the robbers?" Notice Jesus has inverted the lawyer's question. The original question was, "Who *is* my neighbor?" Jesus asks now, "Who *was* a neighbor? Who acted the way a neighbor should act?" The lawyer, unable even to say the word "Samaritan," can only muster, "The one who showed him mercy." He's correct again. Jesus affirms his reply by urging him to go, and do likewise. Jesus shows the lawyer that you're a neighbor if you show mercy. "It is no longer whether the victim of the highway robbery could be considered legally a 'neighbor' to either the priest, the levite [sic], or the Samaritan, but rather which one of them acted as a 'neighbor' to the

---

20. Caird, *Saint Luke*, 148.

unfortunate victim."[21] The neighbor, Jesus explains, is not so much the object of kindness as he is the one who shows kindness. Darrell Bock puts it like this: "If we seek to restrict those we serve, we need to hear the lesson Jesus taught the lawyer. The issue is not who we may or may not serve, but serving where need exists. We are not to seek to limit whom our neighbors might be. Rather, we are to be a neighbor to those whose needs we can meet."[22]

Neighbor love, then, is love in action toward another person. The neighbor in the parable of the Good Samaritan is, in the words of the lawyer, the one who showed mercy. So, we can rightly think of neighbor love as synonymous with the demonstration of mercy. It is compassionate action to meet the needs of those in need. It looks less upon others as our neighbors (though it surely does that) and more upon ourselves and our role and responsibilities as a neighbor to those around us, and particularly to those on the fringes of society whom the world treats unjustly. Neighbor love, then, is not only synonymous with mercy, it's also intertwined with justice, and justice, Miroslav Volf says, involves "render[ing] to each person his or her due" and "seek[ing] their good."[23] He observes:

> A world of perfect justice is a world of love. It is a world with no "rules," in which everyone does what he or she pleases and all are pleased by what everyone does; a world of no "rights" because there are no wrongs from which to be protected; a world of no "legitimate entitlements," because everything is given and nothing withheld; a world with no "equality" because all differences are loved in their own appropriate way. . . . In short, a world of perfect justice would be a world of *transcendent* justice, because it would be a world of *perfect freedom and love*.[24]

What a glorious vision. That is the biblical vision of neighbor love. A world where people show mercy to each other and genuinely seek one another's good. Neighbor love is the fundamental ethic in the Bible, and as Christians, we have a duty to act neighborly, to show mercy to all, and especially to the vulnerable.

21. Fitzmyer, *Luke*, 884.
22. Bock, *Luke*, 1035.
23. Volf, *Exclusion and Embrace*, 220, 224.
24. Ibid., 223; emphases his.

THE CALL TO NEIGHBOR LOVE

Why is mercy a duty? Why is neighbor love necessary? Why must we work toward a world of perfect justice? All biblical injunctions to love, mercy, and justice are rooted in God's character. He is perfectly merciful and just (Deut 32:4; Pss 33:5; 116:5; 145:17) and he is love (1 John 4:8). Because God is perfect in his justice and mercy, he commands his followers to act justly and mercifully toward one another.

Leviticus 19:9–18 contains a list of requirements for how the Israelites were to treat their neighbors. Included in this list are injunctions for providing for the poor and the sojourner (vv. 9–10), commands against oppressing one's neighbor (v. 13), and the positive call to "love your neighbor as yourself" (v. 18). God clearly has a special place in his heart for those in need: "Render true judgments, show kindness and mercy to one another, do not oppress the widow, the fatherless, the sojourner, or the poor, and let none of you devise evil against another in your heart" (Zech 7:9–10).

So important is neighbor love that God rejects the worship of those who fail to show mercy. "I desire mercy and not sacrifice," he says through the prophet Hosea, "the knowledge of God rather than burnt offerings" (Hos 6:6). Jesus quotes these words twice in the gospel of Matthew to say that religious ritual has no value without concern for the needy (9:13; 12:7). As James puts it, "Religion that is pure and undefiled before God the Father" includes "visit[ing] orphans and widows" (1:27). Jesus condemns the hypocrisy of the scribes and Pharisees: "For you tithe mint and dill and cumin, and have neglected the weightier matters of the law: justice and mercy and faithfulness. These you ought to have done, without neglecting the others" (Matt 23:23). It's not that they should have ceased their tithes, Jesus says, but they should have done the more important things the law requires, namely, caring for their neighbors by showing justice and mercy.

The prophet Micah wrote to a community struggling with precisely this issue. In describing the historical background of Micah's prophecy, Waltke says, "A shocking contrast between extreme wealth and poverty was exacerbated by egregious injustices on the part of the élite rich and ruling class against the stalwart landowners, who were driven off their land and into a dependent economic status."[25] In fact, as Waltke

---

25. Waltke, *Micah*, 138.

points out, "Moral corruption was so rife that it even debauched the nation's religious leaders. . . . To be sure the nation looked religious as it thronged the Temple and offered lavish gifts, but the moral covenant, which mandated a loving spirit towards God and one's neighbour, had been replaced by a covenant between the powerful to spoil the poor."[26] In the midst of Micah's prophecy the people ask (6:6–7):

> With what shall I come before the LORD,
>   and bow myself before God on high?
> Shall I come before him with burnt offerings,
>   with calves a year old?
> Will the LORD be pleased with thousands of rams,
>   with ten thousands of rivers of oil?
> Shall I give my firstborn for my transgression,
>   the fruit of my body for the sin of my soul?

The prophet replies (v. 8):

> He has told you, O man, what is good;
>   and what does the LORD require of you
> but to do justice, and to love kindness,
>   and to walk humbly with your God?

God abjectly refused to hear the prayers of his people when they weren't showing neighbor love. Neither sacrifice nor gifts will earn his acceptance; "when we come before God we must remember that it is not so much what is in our hands but what is in our hearts that finds expression in our conduct that is important."[27]

A similar refrain is sounded in Amos 5:21–24. God says through his prophet:

> I hate, I despise your feasts,
>   and I take no delight in your solemn assemblies.
> Even though you offer me your burnt offerings and grain offerings,
>   I will not accept them;
> and the peace offerings of your fattened animals,
>   I will not look upon them.
> Take away from me the noise of your songs;
>   to the melody of your harps I will not listen.
> But let justice roll down like waters,
>   and righteousness like an ever-flowing stream.

26. Ibid., 139.
27. Smith, *Micah-Malachi*, 51.

Alec Motyer says of this text, "There cannot be a passage in the Bible more deliberate in expressing divine distaste than this."[28] These are strong words indeed. If we think God is pleased by our worship when we're not attending to those things that he loves and calls us to care for, Amos says we're in for a rude awakening. God cares very little for our attendance at worship services if we're not attending to our neighbors. God isn't concerned with "ritual punctiliousness."[29] Amos "upbraids in no uncertain terms Israel's extensive ritual praxis, rejecting it in toto: holidays, festal gatherings, and sacrifices, along with their accompanying hymns, melodies, and musical instruments. . . . To all of this ritual mayhem . . . he replies that God demands justice and morality and not the minutiae of the cult: Not rite but right is demanded; devotion not devotions."[30] God does not care a whit for pomp and circumstance. He is not dazzled by how large our churches are or by how well we sing. He wants us to love our neighbors. "Ritual per se, with all its paraphernalia and panoply, simply cannot substitute for the basic moral and ethical actions of humans. When these are lacking, religious life, with all its ritual accoutrements, becomes a sham."[31] Religion is dead without action. When our worship isn't accompanied by acts of neighbor love, God is repulsed (Isa 1:10–17). He doesn't want empty religion. What the Bible makes plain is that religious exercises devoid of merciful action, done without a concern for justice, are futile. They earn us wrath, not blessing. Neighbor love is required of all who profess faith in the living God.

In his magisterial study of justice, philosopher Nicholas Wolterstorff concludes that the Old Testament writers weren't concerned with proving that justice requires care for the marginal, they simply assumed this was so. The biblical prophets and psalmists "take for granted that justice requires alleviating the plight of the lowly. They save their breath for urging their readers to actually *practice* justice to the quartet of the vulnerable ones [widows, orphans, resident aliens, and the poor]."[32]

In the New Testament we find similar injunctions for showing mercy. Both Paul and James agree, for instance, that all the law is summed up with the command to neighbor love (Rom 13:9; Gal 5:14; Jas 2:8). In

28. Motyer, *Day of the Lion*, 131.
29. McComiskey, *Minor Prophets*, 432.
30. Paul, *Amos*, 188.
31. Ibid., 192.
32. Wolterstoff, *Justice*, 76; emphasis his. Today, we might add to this list the unborn, the severely disabled, and the post-autonomous elderly.

his letter to the church in Rome, the Apostle Paul calls each Christian to "please his neighbor for his good, to build him up" and to "welcome one another as Christ has welcomed you, for the glory of God" (Rom 15:2, 7). Christians, Paul says, are to "Bear one another's burdens" (Gal 6:2) and "in humility [to] count others more significant than yourselves" (Phil 2:3). Jesus identifies with the vulnerable and oppressed by becoming, himself, a vulnerable human being; the unjust victim of oppression. In the last day, Jesus says, he will know who rightfully belongs to him based on how we treated the hungry, the thirsty, the stranger, the naked, the sick, and the prisoner while we were alive. In a remarkable passage, Jesus says when we care for the needy we care for him, and when we ignore the needy we ignore him (Matt 25:31–46). There can be no mistake: neighbor love is fundamental to genuine Christian living. We act unjustly anytime we depart from the way God would have us treat one another. The overwhelming conclusion of the Bible is that we owe neighbor love to those in need. Another way to put this is to say that those in need have a right to the mercy that the Samaritan showed the man on the road to Jericho (see Galatians 6:10). It's our responsibility as Christians.[33]

CONCLUSION

We see, then, the relevance that the command to neighbor love has for how we are to treat the unborn. We're forbidden from limiting the scope of our mercy. Just as Jesus told the lawyer that the right question isn't "Who is my neighbor?" but "Will you prove to be a neighbor to all in need?" so, too, the issue with abortion must not be, "Is the unborn a

---

33. I don't have adequate space to attend to the important matter of our motivation for neighbor love. As preachers, we all know that there are lots of wrong reasons for doing good deeds. The Bible tells us repeatedly, and in a variety of forms, that the gospel is the only proper motivation for the demonstration of neighbor love. In the gospel we learn of our own vulnerability, our own need for rescuing, and find that Jesus came to save us. We learn that he became vulnerable for our sake, suffering unjustly, and ultimately dying on the cross for our sins. When we see and believe that Jesus did this for us, though we were (and remain) completely undeserving, we're stirred to help those in need. It is the inevitable conclusion of a gospel-changed heart, and it is a proof of the genuineness of our profession of faith. The gospel is our ultimate motivation for loving our neighbors, and as we come to understand more of its implications, we begin to see others the way God sees them.

That the gospel both requires and motivates us to show mercy has been very ably articulated by Keller in *Ministries of Mercy*. For a stirring meditation on neighbor love, see the great Puritan Richard Baxter's sermon, "Cases and Directions," 870–73.

person?" It is! But, as Hays astutely observes, when Christians ask this question we're doing exactly what the lawyer did when he asked Jesus, "Who is my neighbor?" And Jesus says that's the wrong question. Hays concludes:

> The point is not that the unborn child is by definition a 'neighbor.' Rather, the point is that we are called upon to *become* neighbors to those who are helpless, going beyond conventional conceptions of duty to provide life-sustaining aid to those whom we might not have regarded as worthy of our compassion. . . . When we ask, "Is the fetus a person?" we are asking the same sort of limiting, self-justifying question that the lawyer asked Jesus: "Who is my neighbor?" . . . To define the unborn child as a nonperson is to narrow the scope of moral concern, whereas Jesus calls upon us to widen it by showing mercy and actively intervening on behalf of the helpless. The Samaritan is a paradigm of love that goes beyond ordinary obligation and thus *creates* a neighbor relation where none existed before.[34]

Friends, genuinely obeying the biblical command to neighbor love means interceding on behalf of the unborn. There's simply no other conclusion.

---

34. Hays, *Moral Vision*, 451; emphasis his.

3

What Has the Church Said?

*It is a great wickedness to stifle the child in the womb
when it is newly conceived.*

—JEREMIAH BURROUGHS

IN PREACHING AGAINST ABORTION we need to know both the issue and how Scripture informs our thinking about it. But we also do well to listen to the voices of saints who've come before us. We should know our church history. Why should we care about what the church has historically said about abortion? New Testament scholar Bruce Metzger says:

> The study of the thinking and practice of the early church, though often neglected by modern Protestants, frequently provides the Christian today with valuable insights and information. For one thing, such study deepens one's appreciation of the strength of religious convictions that enabled believers of that age to stand firmly against conforming to the ethics and mores of the surrounding culture. Especially noteworthy in this respect was the opposition of the early church to contemporary practices of abortion. It is really remarkable how uniform and how pronounced was the early Christian opposition to abortion.[1]

It is wise to learn from our ancestors in the faith. They wrestled with the same sorts of things we're wrestling with today, and to ignore what they might have to teach us is shortsighted, foolish, and prideful. We ought to be certain of the strength of our reasons for ever deviating from a long-held position.

---

1. Metzger, Foreword to Gorman, *Abortion and Early Church*, 9.

When we appeal to the ethical beliefs that Christians have traditionally held, we remind our congregations that we are part of a historic faith with a rich well of practical wisdom from which to draw. We learn what other preachers have said about abortion in their day and how they confronted the challenges with which they were faced in their particular contexts. We are emboldened by their courageous example. We profit from the echo of their voices.

EARLY CHRISTIAN WRITINGS

Metzger's claim that Christian opposition to abortion was consistent is well documented by Michael Gorman.[2] The earliest extracanonical Christian writings that oppose abortion are found in the *Didache* and the *Epistle of Barnabas* (although extant Jewish wisdom literature from the Second Temple period also shows an anti-abortion worldview).[3]

The *Didache*, a first century "handbook of church morals, rituals, and discipline . . . offers the oldest explicit Christian instance of the prohibition of abortion."[4] In the first section of the text we read a lengthy list

---

2. I'm indebted to Gorman, *Abortion and Early Church*, for pointing me to many of the primary sources I cite in this following section. See, also, Di Mauro, *Love for Life*.

3. See, for instance, Pseudo-Phocylides 184–85: "Do not let a woman destroy the unborn babe in her belly, nor after its birth throw it before the dogs and the vultures as a prey" (see, also, Philo, *Spec. Laws* 3.108–19; Josephus, *Ag. Ap.* 2.202; *Sib. Or.* 2:281–2). This translation is van der Horst's in "Pseudo-Phocylides." He says of these verses, "Abortion and exposure of children were the current methods of family planning in pagan antiquity" (580n. i).

4. Niederwimmer, *Didache*, 2, 89–90. Subsequent quotations from the *Didache* are from his translation. Although this is the oldest explicit reference to a Christian prohibition against abortion, Niederwimmer adds, "it is certain from the beginning, Christians, following Old Testament and Jewish custom, rejected abortion" (90). Milavec draws the same conclusion in his massive commentary on the *Didache*: "All in all . . . the *Didache* represents the first Christian statement opposing abortion and infanticide. In so doing, however, the *Didache* . . . does not rely on any new teaching of Jesus. Rather, the Christian sources merely embrace the prevailing Jewish reverence for human life: (a) anyone deliberately aborting a formed fetus (using drugs or surgery) extinguishes a human life; (b) anyone exposing a newborn infant risks becoming a murderer" (*Didache*, 142). The horrible practice of exposure (a method of infanticide) is described by Philo in *Special Laws* 3.113–15: "For no one is so foolish as to suppose that those who have treated dishonourably their own flesh and blood will deal honourably with strangers. As to the charges of murder in general and murder of their own children in particular the clearest proofs of their truth is supplied by the parents. Some of them do the deed with their own hands; with monstrous cruelty and barbarity they stifle and throttle the first breath which the infants draw or throw them into a river or into the depths of the

of proscriptions, among which is the command, "You shall not murder a child, whether by abortion or by killing it once it is born" (2.2). There is no confusion. The unborn fetus is a child and abortion is murder.

The *Epistle of Barnabas*, an anonymous letter likely written between AD 70–132 and later connected with the historical Barnabas, contains a similar injunction against abortion: "You shall not abort a child nor, again, commit infanticide" (19.5).[5] Gorman observes that in its immediate context this command follows a command to neighbor love, so that "The fetus is seen, not as part of its mother, but as a neighbor. Abortion is rejected as contrary to other-centered neighbor love."[6] He is surely correct in concluding:

> The significance of these two writings [the *Didache* and the *Epistle of Barnabas*] lies both in their firm position on abortion as murder and in their development of an ethical context within which abortion should be viewed. . . . Furthermore, abortion is depicted not only as a sin like sexual immorality, but as an evil no less severe and social in scope than oppression of the poor and needy and no less dishonorable than the use of poisons.[7]

If the earliest Christian witness was united in condemning abortion as murder, as the *Didache*, the *Epistle of Barnabas*, and other sources suggest,[8] later Christian thinkers and leaders were no less unified in their adamant denunciation of it. The best way I know to show this to you is to let them speak in their own voice.

---

sea, after attaching some heavy substance to make them sink more quickly under its weight. Others take them to be exposed in some desert place, hoping, they themselves say, that they may be saved, but leaving them in actual truth to suffer the most distressing fate. For all the beasts that feed on human flesh visit the spot and feast unhindered on the infants, a fine banquet provided by their sole guardians, those who above all others should keep them safe, their fathers and mothers" (547, 549).

5. This translation is from Holmes, ed., *Apostolic Fathers in English*, 196.
6. Gorman, *Abortion and Early Church*, 49.
7. Ibid., 50.
8. Among the other sources cited by Gorman from the first three centuries AD are the *Apocalypse of Peter* 26; Clement of Alexandria, *Extracts from the Prophets* 41, 48–49; and Athenagoras, *Legatio pro Christianis* 35. There are, in fact, no extant early Christian writings depicting any other attitude toward abortion.

THE CHURCH FATHERS

Tertullian, the brilliant second century Latin church father, has this to say:

> For us murder is once for all forbidden; so even the child in the womb, while yet the mother's blood is still being drawn on to form the human being, it is not lawful for us to destroy. To forbid birth is only quicker murder. It makes no difference whether one take away the life once born or destroy it as it comes to birth. He is a man, who is to be a man; the fruit is always present in the seed.[9]

Tertullian is clear. Just because the fetus is still dependent on the mother for its life doesn't make it any less human. Abortion, he says, is nothing less than murder.

While some early church leaders were hesitant to condemn the aborting of "unformed" fetuses (that is, those they believed did not yet have souls), Basil, bishop of Caesarea, was among those who believed abortion to be murder at every stage of the unborn child's development. In a letter to Amphilochius, bishop of Iconium, Basil says, "She who has deliberately destroyed a fetus has to pay the penalty of murder. And there is no exact inquiry among us as to whether the fetus was formed or unformed."[10] (In fact, Basil says, the woman who has an abortion is guilty of both the murder of the embryo and her own attempted murder, "because usually the women die in such attempts."[11])

John Chrysostom, the "golden mouthed" preacher from the fourth century, had a similar view about the depravity of abortion. In a sermon on Romans 13:11–14, Chrysostom not only condemns abortion, but calls it worse than murder. "For I have no name to give it, since it does not take off the thing born, but prevent its being born. Why then do you abuse the gift of God, and fight with His laws, and follow after what is a curse as if a blessing, and make the chamber of procreation a chamber for murder, and arm the woman that was given for childbearing unto slaughter?"[12] The unborn child is more defenseless than any other person at any other stage in their physical development. She's completely dependent on her mother for life and for the sustaining of life. But it is precisely her mother who is trying to kill her.

---

9. Tertullian, *Apology* 9.8, 49; see, also, Tertullian, *The Soul* 27.
10. Basil, *Letter* 188.2, 12.
11. Ibid., 13.
12. Chrysostom, "Homily 24 on Romans."

THE PROTESTANT REFORMERS

The church's denunciation of abortion continued during the Reformation. In his commentary on Genesis, Martin Luther attributed the prevalence of "girls . . . who prevent conception and kill and expel tender fetuses" to "the wickedness of human nature."[13] Abortion, for Luther, is an evil act by corrupt and sinful people. Elsewhere he urges men to care for their pregnant wives: "For those who have no regard for pregnant women and who do not spare the tender fruit are murderers and infanticides. Thus some men are actually so cruel that they beat those who are heavy with child."[14] While not addressing abortion here, per se, Luther saw the abhorrence of those who fail to protect the unborn. If a man is called cruel for beating a pregnant woman, how much worse is the one who urges the abortion of his own child?

Like Luther, John Calvin was equally aghast at the practice of abortion. In his commentary on the last four books of the Torah, he says, in a note on Exodus 21:22:

> the foetus, though enclosed in the womb of its mother, is already a human being . . . and it is almost a monstrous crime to rob it of the life which it has not yet begun to enjoy. If it seems more horrible to kill a man in his own house than in a field, because a man's house is his place of most secure refuge, it ought surely to be deemed more atrocious to destroy a foetus in the womb before it has come to light.[15]

Calvin's words are reminiscent of both Tertullian's and Chrysostom's. Like Tertullian, Calvin emphasizes the humanity of the fetus. And like Chrysostom, Calvin considers abortion an offense worse than murder. The womb ought to be a place of safety and protection for the unborn baby. But in the case of abortion, what ought to be a sanctuary becomes a slaughterhouse.

KARL BARTH

Karl Barth, one of the most influential Protestant theologians of the twentieth century, also abhorred abortion. He devotes significant space in his massive *Church Dogmatics* to the act he calls "secret and open

---

13. Luther, *Luther's Works*, 4:304–305 (on Genesis 25:1–4).

14. Luther, *What Luther Says*, 905, quoted in part in Schlossberg and Achtemeier, *Not My Own*, 4.

15. Calvin, *Commentaries*, 41–42.

mass murder."[16] First, Barth says, it is not simply the women who choose abortion who are guilty of sin. The net of guilt is cast far wider:

> The persons concerned are the mother who either carries out the act or desires or permits it, the more or less informed amateurs who assist her, perhaps the scientifically and technically trained physician, the father, relatives or other third parties who allow, promote, assist or favour the execution of the act and therefore share responsibility, and in a wider but no less strict sense the society whose conditions and mentality directly or indirectly call for such acts and whose laws may even permit them. . . . Our first contention must be that no pretext can alter the fact that the whole circle of those concerned is in the strict sense engaged in the killing of human life. For the unborn child is from the very first a child. It is still developing and has no independent life. But it is a man and not a thing, nor a mere part of the mother's body.[17]

His words are enough to bring us to our knees, weeping in repentance. We are all guilty of sin where abortion is concerned, according to Barth. By participating in a society that tells women abortion is morally permissible and legally allowable; by living in such a way that suggests individual freedom and rights trump personal responsibility; by not offering enough assistance to pregnant women in need: we are guilty as sin.

This guilt is amplified, Barth continues, when we consider that to even advocate for abortion choice is to put oneself in God's place—to give oneself power that only God rightfully has:

> Those directly or indirectly involved [in abortion] cannot escape this responsibility. . . .
>
> Can we accept [it]? May this thing be? Must it be? Whatever arguments may be brought against the birth and existence of the child, is it his fault that he is here? What has he done to his mother or any of the others that they wish to deprive him of his germinating life and punish him with death? Does not his utter defencelessness and helplessness, or the question whom they are destroying, to whom they are denying a future even before he has breathed and seen the light of the world, wrest the weapon from the hand of his mother first, and then from all the others, thwarting their will to use it? . . . And yet they want to kill him deliberately because certain reasons which have nothing to do with the child himself favour the view that he had better not be born![18]

16. Barth, *Church Dogmatics* III.4, 90.
17. Ibid., 88–89.
18. Ibid.

For Barth, abortion is a monstrous and inexcusable crime. When people seek to justify abortion they need to recognize that the real victim is the unborn baby. The pregnancy may be unwanted, the pregnant woman or couple may live a life of poverty, but these are not the baby's fault. Abortion punishes the unborn child for reasons out of her control.

DIETRICH BONHOEFFER

Barth's contemporary, the Lutheran pastor-theologian Dietrich Bonhoeffer, most well-known for his staunch opposition of Hitler and his execution at the hands of the Nazis, also condemns abortion because it destroys God's creative work. In his *Ethics* he writes:

> To kill the fruit in the mother's womb is to injure the right to life that God has bestowed on the developing life. Discussion of the question whether a human being is already present confuses the simple fact that, in any case, God wills to create a human being and that the life of this developing human being has been deliberately taken. And this is nothing but murder.[19]

In other words, Bonhoeffer, like Barth, sees the choice of abortion as setting oneself up to be God—even above God. Asking whether or not the fetus is a human being is a mistake, he argues. The question we should be asking is what God is intending to create. And there can be no doubt that he is creating a human being. Abortion, then, is destroying God's creative, life-giving act. Regardless of whether we define this as taking life or depriving life, Bonhoeffer says, abortion is murder.

MOTHER TERESA

In a sermon at the National Prayer Breakfast in Washington, DC, Mother Teresa said, "I feel that the greatest destroyer of peace today is abortion, because it is a war against the child, a direct killing of the innocent child, murder by the mother herself."[20] Like Bonhoeffer and others, Mother Teresa is unequivocal in naming abortion as murder. This, she says, is tragic, both for the mother who "does not learn to love, but kills even her own child to solve her problems," and for the father, who "is told that he does not have to take any responsibility at all for the child he has brought

---

19. Bonhoeffer, *Ethics*, 206.
20. Mother Teresa, "Whatever You Did," 104.

into the world."²¹ Abortion is a sin because the "unborn child has been carved in the hand of God from conception and is called by God to love and to be loved, not only now in this life, but forever."²² When we abort our babies and allow abortion to continue, we destroy God's creative work and fail in a most catastrophic way to love one whom he has called us to love. Instead of abortion, Mother Teresa pleads with men and women to give their unwanted children up for adoption, to those who do want them: "Please don't kill the child. I want the child. Please give me the child. I am willing to accept any child who would be aborted and to give that child to a married couple who will love the child and be loved by the child."²³ Would that such words spring from our own lips.

POPE JOHN PAUL II

Though many other examples from the Christian tradition could be marshaled in support of the claim that the church has always opposed abortion, one final example will have to suffice. Let's consider Pope John Paul II's encyclical letter *Evangelium Vitae* (*The Gospel of Life*).²⁴

He says, "Among all the crimes which can be committed against life, procured abortion has characteristics making it particularly serious and deplorable."²⁵ Among these characteristics is the helplessness and utter dependency of the unborn baby on her mother. "He or she [i.e., the unborn child] is *weak*, defenceless, even to the point of lacking that minimal form of defence consisting in the poignant power of a newborn baby's cries and tears. The unborn child is *totally entrusted* to the protection and care of the woman carrying him or her in the womb."²⁶

Pope John Paul II warns us of the increasing acceptance of abortion and what it means to us as a civilization, and he encourages us to be bold and uncompromising in our stand against it:

> The acceptance of abortion in the popular mind, in behaviour and even in law itself, is a telling sign of an extremely dangerous crisis of the moral sense, which is becoming more and more

---

21. Ibid., 104–5.
22. Ibid., 105.
23. Ibid., 106.
24. John Paul II, *Gospel of Life*; see especially sections 58–63 (in chapter 3).
25. Ibid., 103.
26. Ibid., 104; emphases his.

incapable of distinguishing between good and evil, even when the fundamental right to life is at stake. Given such a grave situation, we need now more than ever to have the courage to look the truth in the eye and to *call things by their proper name*, without yielding to convenient compromises or to the temptation of self-deception. In this regard the reproach of the Prophet is extremely straightforward: "Woe to those who call evil good and good evil, who put darkness for light and light for darkness" (Is 5:20).[27]

Would that we preachers hear and heed the Pope's words.

CONCLUSION

For more than nineteen hundred years the church was virtually undivided in understanding and treating abortion as a heinous sin. In recent decades, however, there has been a marked divergence. While many denominations continue to uphold the historic Christian view that abortion is murder, other Christian groups have become unapologetically pro-choice.[28] Within the church, then, are those who call evil good and good evil. This is a sad shift from the moral and biblical position of the church historic. What's needed is a return to our roots. And this return must begin in the pulpit.

We ignore the voices of wise Christians from church history to our peril and society's loss. When the church has been as united as it has been on an issue like abortion, we do well to listen and tell our people. We who preach should remember those who've come before us and learn from this "great cloud of witnesses" (Heb 12:1). We should stand upon their shoulders and in their pulpits and tell our generation what the church has always declared about abortion.

---

27. Ibid., 103–4; emphasis his.

28. Take a look at the dated but still telling compilation of official church statements in Melton, *Churches Speak On Abortion*. He summarizes: "The positions taken by religious groups have fallen fairly consistently along the conservative/liberal lines established for other topics. For example, a Christian church that is conservative in its theology (i.e., promotes a literal interpretation of the Bible) has likely taken conservative positions on other social topics and will almost certainly be against abortion. A Christian church with a liberal theology (i.e., promotes a more contextual or metaphoric interpretation of the Bible) has likely taken liberal positions on other social topics and will tend to take a pro-choice stance on abortion" (xvi).

PART TWO

Who's Preaching, Who's Listening

4

Abortion and the Preacher

Not only for every idle word but for every idle silence must man render an account.

—Saint Ambrose

Those called to the preaching vocation wield great power. Preachers are entrusted with the proclamation of the gospel, the power of God by which people are saved (Rom 1:16; 10:14). As we expound God's Word from week to week, we have tremendous influence over our congregations. Our words have the capacity to shape the beliefs of our hearers. For many Christians, we are the foremost Bible scholars they know—maybe the only one they know—and an authority on all spiritual matters. Their understanding of God and themselves will be formed, in no small part, by what they hear from the pulpit. What we say about the place of mercy ministry and social concern will likely have a significant impact on what our people think and do, and what programs our churches spearhead and participate in.

In light of the task to which we're called, we simply cannot stay silent when it comes to the unborn. How can we, when abortion "is dismembering, scraping, and sucking out from the womb the lives of millions of children"[1] in our own neighborhoods? Silence is simply not an option. Prenatal children are counting on us to live up to our calling. "We are preachers and people in the Church of a resurrected Lord," reminds Elizabeth Achtemeier, "a Lord who willed life for us—not the death of an abortion clinic. That wanton slaughter is almost unspeakable in our time, but speak to it from our pulpits we must. For we preachers

---

1. Achtemeier, "Speaking the Unspeakable," 26.

have been given the task of speaking always about the God of life and the gospel of life."[2] I pray that you would be bold and unwavering in preaching to defend the life of the unborn.

PROPHETIC PREACHING

Some call preaching on controversial social and moral issues like abortion *prophetic preaching*. This doesn't mean that contemporary preachers are prophets exactly like Jeremiah and Amos. John Stott makes this very plain when he says that the preacher "does not derive his message from God as a direct and original revelation. . . . No original revelation is given to him; his task is to expound the revelation which has been given once for all. . . . Now that the written word of God is available to us all, the word of God in prophetic utterance is no longer needed."[3] Instead, what we mean by the term *prophetic preaching* is pleading the case of the marginalized and oppressed, often to those who are, at best, unaware or disinterested, and at worst, directly complicit in their involvement.[4] It is "out of season" preaching (2 Tim 4:2). Because prophetic preaching means different things to different people, here are five clarifying statements about how I understand and envision the task today.

First, *prophetic preaching is preaching*. By this I mean that it is not simply a public lecture or an ethical talk or an inspiring message urging action on behalf of some social cause. It is preaching, and as such, must conform to the norms of preaching. So, we preach from the Bible, or more specifically, from some text of the Bible, and we make as the idea of our sermon the idea of that text.[5] We preach not our own ideas or opinions, but truth that comes from the Word of God. This means when we preach on abortion we aren't telling our people our opinion that abortion is sinful; our opinion is inconsequential. Why should anyone care what we think, unless what we think is biblical and true? God's

2. Ibid.

3. Stott, *Preacher's Portrait*, 11–13.

4. Stott says the term is an unhelpful one, that it leads to confusion and abuse. Perhaps he is right, in which case what is needed is new terminology and nomenclature. However, homiletics professor David Schnasa Jacobsen, though agreeing that "The institutions of prophecy, whether in the Hebrew Bible or the New Testament, are long gone," nevertheless argues that "the 'prophetic' as a mode of preaching is still with us" ("*Schola Prophetarum*," 18–19).

5. See, for instance, Chapell, *Christ-Centered Preaching*; Robinson, *Biblical Preaching*; Wilson, *Four Pages*.

Word must always govern prophetic preaching as it does all preaching, and our words from the pulpit must always be subject and captive to scriptural truth.

Second, *prophetic preaching is gospel-rooted and Christ-centered*. Our prophetic sermons must always, always lead people to see Jesus (John 12:21; 1 Cor 1:23; 2:2). In other words, our sermons must be Christian sermons.[6] They must hold out the gospel and seek to lead people to glorify God. Ultimately, we pray that God will be pleased to use our preaching to change lives. Transformation is essential. Without this concern and focus, our preaching is reduced to mere moral exhortation. There's nothing wrong with telling people what to do and what not to do, but when this is divorced from God's justifying and sanctifying grace—when it's separated from the gospel, the need for conversion, and the marks of sanctification—our moral deeds are meaningless. Our people wrongly think that their virtuous actions merit them God's favor. Paul tells us, on the contrary, "Whatever does not proceed from faith is sin" (Rom 14:23). Preaching for transformation is essential to prophetic preaching. And what leads to transformation but a message centered on Christ and his gospel?

Third, *prophetic preaching is pastoral in nature*. We don't speak of prophetic preaching as though it were something different, or distinct, from regular pastoral preaching. No such dichotomy exists. All of our preaching is pastoral in nature. All of our preaching is crucial to the task of shepherding the flock. Prophetic preaching specifically advocates for one or more vulnerable groups, but it's no less pastoral for doing so. Paul Scott Wilson says:

> For Jesus, pastor and prophet were one: we cannot separate Jesus' teachings into those about social justice and those about pastoral care.... Could we say that the story of the Good Samaritan was more pastoral care than social justice? Both were interwoven. Both were held in tension. They were both part of his overriding concern for the weighty measures of the law—justice, mercy, and love. For they cannot be alternatives either.[7]

---

6. Jay Adams says, "If you preach a sermon that would be acceptable to the members of a Jewish synagogue or to a Unitarian congregation, there is something radically wrong with it. Preaching, when truly Christian, is *distinctive*. And what makes it distinctive is the all-pervading presence of a saving and sanctifying Christ. Jesus Christ must be at the heart of every sermon you preach" (*Preaching With Purpose*, 147; emphasis his).

7. Wilson, *Imaginations of the Heart*, 191. It should be noted that neither Wilson

When we preach prophetically, at the very least, we "raise the consciousness of the church [and] make people intensely and often uncomfortably aware of issues."[8] By bringing issues like abortion to our people's consciousness and conscience, and by calling them to repent and act, we fulfill our role as shepherds of the people whom God has entrusted to us. Some women in our congregations need to repent for having had an abortion; they need to hear and receive God's forgiveness and love. Some men need to repent for encouraging their girlfriends, wives, sisters, and daughters to abort. All of us need to repent for being indirectly complicit in the abortion culture by having embraced the Western idol of radical individualism. All of us need to repent for being active agents in a social system that permits the killing of the unborn. All of us need to repent for not bearing more of the burdens that women in crisis pregnancies have to shoulder largely on their own. When we name abortion as sin, call people to repentance, hold out the offer of forgiveness in Christ, and urge people to act in gospel-rooted boldness, we do prophetic work, but this is nothing less than the essence of pastoral care.

Fourth, *prophetic preaching is hard*. Let's not think that naming abortion as a sin will be easy. There will be listeners in our congregations who have had abortions in the past; who know family members who have had abortions; who may simply feel guilty over having once considered having an abortion. There will be those who are pro-choice, unreceptive to our words, and even angry with us. We may hear from others who complain that we're becoming distracted by something less important than the proclamation of the gospel. We may hear from people who wonder why we don't give more attention to some other social cause. No, prophetic preaching is anything but easy. You may find your own heart growing weary and deflated as you learn more about abortion. Preaching against abortion, like all prophetic preaching, is hard.

But fifth, *prophetic preaching is needed*. As hard as preaching against abortion is, it is necessary. As preachers we "have considerable potential as opinion leaders. Clergy are endowed with varying degrees of authority in pronouncements in certain matters, and, through the ser-

---

nor several other authors I cite in this chapter make explicitly clear whether or not they are in agreement with the pro-life position I defend throughout this book. While I reference their work on ethics, generally, such references should not, therefore, be seen as necessarily suggestive of their views on abortion, specifically.

8. Sisk, *Preaching Ethically*, 111.

mon, have the opportunity to attempt to influence lay attitudes."[9] When well over one million babies are killed *in utero* each year in Canada and the United States and we don't say anything about it to our people, we commit a tragic sin of omission. Neighbor love demands that we plead their case. We must be the voice of the voiceless. The Old Testament prophets serve as role models for us in this. They "talked about all aspects of life. They had things to say about money, sex, and power. They did not avoid attacking issues of worship, war, or women. They were not afraid to condemn power-hungry kings, dishonest court officials, gouging landlords, or wicked priests."[10] How would Isaiah or Jeremiah or Ezekiel react if they lived in our day? How might Jesus? We don't need to speculate. We don't need to guess. Jesus has already shown us what he would do precisely in what he did do for us. We were vulnerable, lost, and in need of saving, and he "gave himself for our sins to rescue us" (Gal 1:4). Today, the unborn need rescuing. We can't do anything to get them "born again," but there is so much we can do to help them be born a first time. We can't rescue them from the wages of sin, but we can rescue them from death by abortion. We can. We must.

"Where have all the prophets gone?" one writer has asked.[11] In a world filled with injustices, in a nation where unborn babies are legally killed by the thousands each day, the church must respond, and we who preach must call her to action. We must stand against evil.

THE PREACHER'S RESPONSIBILITIES

When we keep quiet on abortion we fail to show neighbor love to the unborn. Where Jesus calls us to imitate the Samaritan, instead, like the priest and the Levite, we fail to live up to our responsibilities. And just what are our responsibilities as preachers? Here are four.

Preach the Gospel

As preachers, our chief task is to proclaim the gospel. But we miss the holistic nature of the gospel if we reduce it merely to personal salvation and individual reconciliation with God. Certainly, these are true and essential, even central, but the gospel is more than that. Moreover,

---

9. Jelen, "Clergy and Abortion," 138.
10. Smith, *Prophets as Preachers*, 342–43.
11. McMickle, *Where Have All the Prophets Gone?*

the gospel is especially good news to the vulnerable. Jesus described his own ministry in terms of service to those on the margins of society: "The Spirit of the Lord is upon me, because he has anointed me to proclaim good news to *the poor*. He has sent me to proclaim liberty to *the captives* and recovery of sight to *the blind*, to set at liberty *those who are oppressed*, to proclaim the year of the Lord's favor" (Luke 4:18–19). "The liberation that Jesus promised was not narrowly individualistic, but broadly social; it was not exclusively spiritual, but also held the promise of tangible blessings."[12] There's a special sense in which the gospel is for our weakest neighbors. So, how do we proclaim this gospel to the vulnerable unborn? We can't do it with words, obviously. We can't speak it to those in the womb. But we can preach to those who need to hear this truth; those who are choosing abortion; those who are indifferent; those who could be doing something but aren't.

When we preach in the prophetic mode—when we preach against abortion—we do so because the gospel, itself, is at stake. Abortion denies something fundamental to it. The gospel calls us to repentance and the confession of sin, but the pro-choice movement treats abortion as a "right." It says that the woman is the sole arbiter of whether or not to carry or kill her child. The gospel requires us to say this is wrong. We are obliged! Wilson says "failure to raise justice issues in preaching is a challenge to the relevancy of the gospel."[13] Achtemeier agrees and wants us preachers to see how this applies to pro-life ministry:

> If we will not proclaim the commandments of God with respect to sex and abortion, then we also cannot proclaim the heart of the gospel—that forgiveness, healing, and new life are available through the Cross and Resurrection of Jesus Christ for us sinners. If there is no sin, there is no need of forgiveness, and Christ died in vain; and we preachers might as well forget the whole task of the pulpit and go sell insurance or do something else that is useful.[14]

We need to name abortion as sin and tell people that this is a sin for which Jesus died and had to die. Abortion, as one pro-life worker wisely observes, is "an act of religious faith. . . . [For the woman who undergoes an abortion] it affirms a belief in man as ultimate rather than as created

---

12. Ryken, *Message of Salvation*, 165.
13. Wilson, *Imaginations of the Heart*, 194.
14. Achtemeier, "Speaking the Unspeakable," 25.

in the image of God. It is a commitment to an alien faith that rivals Christianity at the most fundamental levels."[15] When we fail to preach against abortion, our silence implies that it's not a significant enough concern to warrant our time or attention. That's just not true.[16] Again, the gospel, itself, is at stake.

If we fail to proclaim the gospel, we fail in our primary responsibility as preachers. The Apostle Paul called a curse upon himself if he stumbled in this chief task: "Woe to me if I do not preach the gospel!" (1 Cor 9:16). And so with us. We preachers must remember what it is we preach: the gospel of Jesus Christ. We are his ambassadors (2 Cor 5:20; Eph 6:20).[17] We do well to hear Paul's exhortation to his young colleague Timothy: "Preach the word; be ready in season and out of season; reprove, rebuke, and exhort, with complete patience and teaching" (2 Tim 4:2).[18] This is our primary responsibility. Whether lives are actually transformed is not up to us. We must simply prove faithful to the task of preaching God's Word. As the great pastor-theologian Jonathan Edwards puts it, "The work that we do in preaching the gospel, whether it be effectual or not, is acceptable to God. If we are faithful, our labor is an acceptable offering to God, and he smells a sweet savor in our offering."[19] As preachers, then, we must devote our lives to knowing the gospel and the God of it. New Testament scholar Klyne Snodgrass says, "Pastors must be experts in the gospel—the broadest subject in the world—and its application to life, beginning with themselves."[20] May we hear this charge well.

15. Gilstrap, *Phineas Report*; quoted in Walton, *Biblical Solutions*, 8–9.

16. Frank Pavone says, "Those in the pain of abortion are not helped by silence. Some refrain from preaching about abortion out of a sincere motive not to hurt those who have had one. A person grieving over abortion, however, can infer from our silence that we do not know her pain, or that we do not care, or that there is no hope. None of this is true. By our clear and compassionate instruction we can break through the silence that led her to this disastrous choice in the first place.

"People need to know that abortion is their business. Many lament abortion but do not try to stop it. Many are pro-life in the sense that they would never have or encourage an abortion. But neither would many try to stop someone else from having one" ("Talking Abortion").

17. For a scholarly treatment of this Pauline metaphor for preaching, see Bash, *Ambassadors for Christ*.

18. For "gospel" and "word" as synonymous, see Pahl, "'Gospel' and 'Word,'" 211–27.

19. Edwards, "Gospel Ministers," 205. This is Edwards's paraphrase of 2 Corinthians 2:15.

20. Snodgrass, *Ephesians*, 225.

If and when you find yourself growing discouraged, consider the words of 2 Corinthians 8:18. The Apostle Paul, writing to introduce his associate Titus to the church in Corinth, briefly alludes to another companion on the journey. "With [Titus] we are sending the brother who is famous among all the churches for his preaching of the gospel." What an encouraging testimony. Here was a man famous in his day for one thing: preaching the good news. And yet, today his name is lost to us. His identity is completely unknown, save for these few brief words about him. He's been forever immortalized in Scripture, though he's nameless and faceless. But God used him and his message of the saving work of Christ to change lives in his day.

We, too, must go about the same business of proclaiming the gospel in our day and not shrink back. Let's tell our people "the whole counsel of God" (Acts 20:27). When this "counsel" tells us to defend the vulnerable and rescue those about to be killed, we need to teach it. When we preach on abortion, then, we must show how it's connected with the gospel. When we fail to preach the gospel—when we fail to connect our exhortation to morality with the saving work of Christ—we're not just being unfaithful to our calling as preachers, but unfaithful to the gospel, itself.

Protect the Sheep

A second responsibility we have as preachers is to protect our congregations. The image of the pastor as a shepherd defending his flock of sheep from the wolves is a recurring metaphor in Scripture (Matt 9:36; John 10:11; Acts 20:28–31; 1 Pet 5:1–4).

When it comes to abortion, the responsibility to protect the sheep means at least two things. First, we must protect our congregations from false teachers. We live in an age where many who bear the mantle of Christian leadership fail to say anything about the sin of abortion, with some even suggesting its legitimacy as an option. Perhaps worse still, some sound downright holy. On closer inspection, though, they prove to be wolves in sheep's clothing. A prime example is a group called *Progressive Christians Uniting*. John Cobb, a member of this group, says:

> The rhetoric of the pro-life group is overblown when it implies that with the fertilization of an ovum there is a human person. Nevertheless, its passionate commitment to the cause of the fetus is an important reminder that we are dealing with a potential human being. Christians should be gravely hesitant to destroy

the rich potentialities embodied in a fetus. The opposition to abortion has strong grounds here. Nevertheless, even when we approach matters entirely from the perspective of the fetus, there are occasions when abortion may be indicated.[21]

He goes on to cite extreme deformity and unwantedness as instances where abortion may be justified.

There's much here that demands comment. Cobb says "the pro-life group is overblown when it implies that with the fertilization of an ovum there is a human person . . . [but] we are dealing with a potential human being." This is a common argument, but it must be asked, if the fetus is simply "a potential human being," that is, if it is not yet a human person, what is it? Was Jesus merely a potential Messiah, potentially the Lord, when he was in Mary's womb? Size and degree of development must not be the indicators by which we adjudicate whether another is "a human person" or not. In contrast to this claim that the fetus isn't a person or a human being, Ronald Sider says, "The ever-clearer scientific evidence is indisputable. From the moment of conception, we have a genetically distinct being who grows without any biological break to become the baby whom at birth almost everyone still today accepts as a human being to be protected."[22] In other words, to call the fetus a "potential" human is fraught with error. The fetus is a developing human being, just as a newborn baby is a developing human being. Both are in the process of growing in maturity, but they cannot be said to be anything other, or less, than human persons.

Cobb does recognize that "Christians should be gravely hesitant to destroy the rich potentialities embodied in a fetus," but even here, his language is too soft. He doesn't go far enough. Why should we be merely "hesitant," even if it's "gravely" so? If the fetus isn't a human person, as Cobb suggests, there's no warrant for *not* destroying it. Cobb is absolutely right that there are "rich potentialities embodied in a fetus." But there are also rich potentialities embodied in a baby who's been born. There are rich potentialities embodied in a teenager and, yes, even in one who's retired. The key word here is "embodied." The fetus has a body. It's a small body, to be sure, and it's not yet fully formed, but it *is* a human body—a human life that demands protecting.

21. Cobb Jr., ed., *Progressive Christians Speak*, 47–48.
22. Sider, *Scandal of Evangelical Politics*, 147.

Despite the hesitation that Cobb says is warranted, he does allow for abortions under at least a couple of situations: extreme deformity and unwantedness. This is a very troubling conclusion, and we must protect our people from such teaching. Neither deformity nor wantedness determine whether or not a fetus is human.[23]

Mark Dever and Paul Alexander say:

> A faithful shepherd is always on the watch against predators and will put himself in harm's way on behalf of the flock when the need arises (John 10:12-15). Most of these predators will come in the form of teachers who twist the truth (Acts 20:28-31), which is why pastors and elders are called to be men who can 'encourage others in sound doctrine and refute those who oppose it' (Titus 1:9, NIV).[24]

We've been entrusted with the guardianship of God's beloved children, and we must protect them from false teachers of all kinds.

A second aspect of our responsibility to protect the sheep involves interceding and advocating on behalf of the unborn. Just as Paul urges the Thessalonian Christians to "help the weak" (1 Thess 5:14), so we must plead the case of the defenseless unborn. Though they may not be part of our local congregations, they are within the realm of our responsibility. As Edmund Clowney says, "The minister who stands in the pulpit is ministering to God, the church and the world all at once."[25] We must not restrict our pastoral care and our concern as preachers to the people whose names are on our membership rolls.

The writer of Proverbs 24 calls us to "Rescue those who are being taken away to death; hold back those who are stumbling to the slaughter" (v. 11). He's vague as to what, if any specific injustice he has in mind,

---

23. Cobb doesn't go anywhere near as far as some other professing Christians. Katherine Hancock Ragsdale, an Episcopal priest and the dean and president of Episcopal Divinity School, calls abortion "a blessing" in a sermon titled "Our Work is Not Done." She says, "And when a woman becomes pregnant within a loving, supportive, respectful relationship; has every option open to her; decides she does not wish to bear a child; and has access to a safe, affordable abortion—there is not a tragedy in sight—only blessing. The ability to enjoy God's good gift of sexuality without compromising one's education, life's work, or ability to put to use God's gifts and call is simply blessing." A critique and transcript of this sermon is available online at http://blogs.telegraph.co.uk/news/damianthompson/9363917/Abortion_is_a_blessing_and_abortionists_are_doing_holy_work_says_Anglican_priest/.

24. Dever and Alexander, *Deliberate Church*, 94–95.

25. Clowney, *Called to the Ministry*, 60.

but surely his words apply to abortion. When we tell our people the truth about abortion and call them to repentance and resistance, we participate in the rescue mission to which Scripture calls us.

Care for Souls

A third responsibility with which preachers and leaders are entrusted is to keep watch over the souls of the people under our charge (Heb 13:17). Like John Bunyan's character Great-heart, we are "the guide[s] of these Pilgrims which are going to the Celestial Country."[26] We are undershepherds of the chief Shepherd, though we are sheep, ourselves, in need of his care (1 Pet 5:1–4). Just like the undershepherds in the Bible, our care for souls must include calling people to repentance. It is not only those who have had abortions or who have been vocal in their support of a woman's so-called right to choose who are culpable. We all are.

We must be on guard against an understanding of evil that fails to include societal or systemic sin. Such a view is too narrow. As Wilson says:

> When our understanding of evil, aside from natural evil, is only personal . . . we will be tempted to think of our ministry as primarily pastoral. The doctrine of systemic evil affirms that even if everyone were to turn to God, there would still be evil in the world. Sin resides in social systems, not just in individuals. . . . Individuals participate in systems that deny justice, peace, and love. We all share a responsibility for societal sin.[27]

By centering our lives around our personal autonomy; by not doing enough to help the unborn; by making child rearing the sole responsibility of the parent(s), rather than a community prerogative, we're all culpable. It's radically uncaring not to show people their transgressions. Many of our folks don't see themselves as guilty of sin with respect to abortion. Some believe that simply accepting the pro-life position is enough. But to do nothing is sin. Preachers must call attention to it. Surely the priest and the Levite sinned when they passed by the other side of the road. Not only that, simply to inhabit and participate in social systems that lead women to choose abortion is sin. We are all guilty.

---

26. Bunyan, *Pilgrim's Progress*, 294.
27. Wilson, *Imaginations of the Heart*, 196.

We all stand condemned apart from the saving work of Christ and the righteousness he offers to those who ask God's forgiveness.

John the Baptist called people to "a baptism of repentance for the forgiveness of sins" and urged all who would hear his message to "Bear fruits in keeping with repentance" (Luke 3:3, 8). Notice John expected that repentance—turning from sin and turning to a new way of life in God—would lead to tangible evidence of a new life: "fruits." In Luke 3:11 he proceeds to tell the crowds what these fruits look like: "Whoever has two tunics is to share with him who has none, and whoever has food is to do likewise." In short, repentance shows itself to be true and genuine when it leads to a life poured out in mercy—when it leads to neighbor love. It follows, then, that a lack of neighbor love, a pattern of life more consistent with that of the priest or Levite than the Samaritan, indicates the absence of repentance.

Martin Luther understood this well. The third of his ninety-five theses says, in part, "there is no inward repentance which does not outwardly work divers mortifications of the flesh." Moreover, repentance must be continual. Luther's first thesis is that "the whole life of believers should be repentance."[28] A lack of repentance, the Bible says, brings a curse from Christ (Matt 11:21). It simply won't do to plead ignorance.

The Apostle Paul was no stranger to confronting people in sin. In Galatians 2:11–14 he recounts a time he opposed Peter for his hypocrisy in refusing to eat with uncircumcised Gentiles. Why did Paul rebuke Peter? "Because he stood condemned" (v. 11). He was in spiritual peril. Paul loved Peter and cared for him, and because of his affection, had to confront him over his sin. To let Peter continue in sin—persisting in disobedience, doing damage to himself, to others, and to his relationship with God—would have been the most unloving thing to do.

When we preach the gospel, we need to call people to repentance. This was Jesus' charge to his disciples (Luke 24:46–47). The gospel isn't the gospel when we leave this out. If we love our people and care for their souls, we have to call them to repentance. When we preach the good news, our goal isn't, and can't be, simply for people to feel better about themselves. We tell people the indicative of the gospel: that Jesus lived and died for sinners to reconcile them to God; and we tell them the imperative of the gospel: how we must then live in light of what God did for us.

---

28. Luther, "Power and Efficacy of Indulgences."

Ultimately, the reason we care for the souls of our people is because Christ does. Jesus, the most loving person who ever lived, was constantly rebuking people for their sin and calling them to repentance (Matt 4:17; Luke 5:32). But he rebuked because he loved. And we serve him when we care for our congregations. "Whatever you do," Paul says, "work heartily, as for the Lord and not for men, knowing that from the Lord you will receive the inheritance as your reward. You are serving the Lord Jesus Christ" (Col 3:23–24). We tend to those whom Christ loves and calls us to care for, and we must care for them as he would. If we would be shepherds after God's own heart, we must care for our people and urge them to care for the weakest and most needy among us (Jer 3:15).

Equip the Saints

Another reason we preach and teach is "to equip the saints for the work of ministry" (Eph 4:11–12). The Bible is given "that the man of God may be competent, equipped for every good work" (2 Tim 3:16–17). The reason we were created is "for good works" (Eph 2:10). In his letter to Titus, Paul urges his apprentice to shepherd the congregation in Crete. He tells Titus to remind his people "to be ready for every good work" (3:1) and "to devote themselves to good works" (3:8). What good works does Paul have in mind? He answers this question in verse 14: "Let your people learn to devote themselves to good works, *so as to help cases of urgent need, and not be unfruitful.*"

Friends, hear what he's saying. We are called to equip our congregations to do good, and particularly, to do good to those in urgent need. Not to help is to be unfruitful, and the fate of the unfruitful is tragic (John 15:2, 6). I can think of no one in more urgent need than fetuses on the brink of being aborted. We need to give tools to our people so that they can take action and demonstrate neighbor love.

When we preach God's Word, we "help people be productive with their own Christian service."[29] Christian service is hardly restricted to what takes place in our church buildings on Sunday mornings. The work of the church is the work of the people of God. It is done seven days a week. Our preaching must call people to "be imitators of God," as Paul writes in Ephesians 5, "And walk in love, as Christ loved us and gave himself up for us" (vv. 1–2). We must graciously tell people that they need to show love and do good toward the unborn, and give them prac-

---

29. Snodgrass, *Ephesians*, 225.

tical suggestions on what to do. We must encourage our local churches to join together and "consider how to stir up one another to love and good works" (Heb 10:24).

Throughout the history of the church, we read and hear of believers banding together to help the needy. In the book of Acts, Barnabas sells one of his fields and gives the proceeds to the apostles to distribute to those in need (Acts 4:36–37). Others share what they have with all so that "There was not a needy person among them" (Acts 4:34). This tangible demonstration of love to the most vulnerable continues to this day. As *New York Times* columnist Nicholas Kristof observes, "In parts of Africa where bandits and warlords shoot or rape anything that moves, you often find that the only groups still operating are Doctors Without Borders and religious aid workers: crazy doctors and crazy Christians."[30] If I might offer a slight emendation to Kristof, it's not crazy Christians who willingly risk their lives for others, it's ordinary, obedient ones.

We live in an age where Christian unity and love displayed in sacrificial service continues to be needed. As preachers, we are charged with equipping our people for this work. We must not neglect our responsibility to proclaim the gospel, protect the sheep, care for souls, and equip the saints. These are the God-directed duties of our calling. It is a high and noble task, and one that carries with it immense responsibility (1 Tim 3:1). We dare not shirk from the mission at hand. The Bible tells us that those of us who would be teachers of the gospel will be judged with greater strictness (Jas 3:1). So, devote yourself to preaching the gospel and all its implications, not neglecting what it means for how we treat the least among us, the unborn.

THE CHARACTER OF THE PROPHETIC PREACHER

I pray that you would take up this charge and accept this challenge. Before proceeding, however, it's worth spending some time reflecting on the kind of person you ought to *be* if you are to preach against abortion. Our inner lives—our character, our personal holiness—are of the utmost importance. "For the herald of the gospel to be spiritually out of order in his own proper person is, both to himself and to his work, a most serious calamity," Charles Spurgeon told his preaching students.[31]

---

30. Kristof, "Evangelicals a Liberal Can Love."

31. Spurgeon, *Lectures to My Students*, 8. The whole lecture from which this sen-

Or, as a friend of mine puts it, we can only lead our people as far as we ourselves have gone. In a similar vein, Richard Baxter expresses this warning to fellow ministers:

> Many a preacher is now in hell, who hath a hundred times called upon his hearers to use the utmost care and diligence to escape it. Can any reasonable man imagine that God should save men for offering salvation to others, while they refuse it themselves; and for telling others those truths which they neglect and abuse? Many a tailor goes in rags, that maketh costly clothes for others; and many a cook scarcely licks his fingers, when he hath dressed for others the most costly dishes. . . . Take heed, therefore, to yourselves first, that you be that which you persuade your hearers to be, and believe that which you persuade them to believe, and heartily entertain that Saviour whom you offer to them.[32]

First, then, the prophetic preacher *loves God.* Jonathan Edwards says the minister of the gospel "has his soul enkindled with the heavenly flame; his heart burns with love to Christ, and fervent desires of the advancement of his kingdom and glory; and also with ardent love to the souls of men, and desires for their salvation."[33] There is nothing more important to the life of the preacher than intimacy with God. Time spent with him is requisite for a life of holiness, which is what our people need most from us. I once heard a pastor say, "Do as I say, not as I do," but this was absolutely foreign to the Apostle Paul, who said, in effect, "Do as I say *and* as I do." Only when our lives are God-centered will we be able to say to our people, with Paul, "Follow me, as I follow Christ" (1 Cor 4:16; 11:1). Only when we make God our center and his priorities our priorities will we be able to act toward others the way he desires us to act. The prophetic preacher is one who strives to love God with all his heart, soul, mind, and strength. When we love him, our lives are changed and shaped according to his heart. Nothing we do will be of any real lasting value if we do not plant our lives and ministries on him.

How do you stir your heart to greater affection for God? Immerse yourself in his Word and hear him communicating his love to you. Spend time each day contemplating your great sin and God's great grace. Spend time with other Christians who know and love him. Read books that

---

tence comes is well worth reading ("The Minister's Self-watch," 7–21).

32. Baxter, *Reformed Pastor*, 53–55; quoted in Lim, "*Reformed Pastor*," 152.
33. Edwards, "True Excellency," 92.

enflame your heart for him. And pray. Pray without ceasing (1 Thess 5:17). Pray to God that you might love him more.

Second, the prophetic preacher is *compassionate*. We need to love the unborn with a desperate and sacrificial love. We must love them the way Christ loved us (John 13:34). But we must also love the hurting women and men in our congregations, particularly those struggling with guilt over past abortions. We must hold out to them the good news of God's forgiveness and grace. Remember, when we preach prophetically, we don't cease to preach pastorally. Indeed, the best prophetic preaching is pastoral:

> When pastor and prophet are treated as equal and are in relationship, imagination of the heart is set free. Our prophetic function prevents our ministry from becoming too narrow. Our pastoral function prevents our anger and frustration with the sin of the world from turning into deep-seated bitterness. Together they foster hope and enable us to recognize God's ongoing action in the world that brings us to the fullness of time. Mother Teresa says there are no great acts, just small acts done in great love. Our small attempts to change the world are not small or futile if they are seen as part of the action of Christ's body around the world to bring forth God's will.[34]

By remembering that we are pastors when we preach prophetically, we will remember to have compassion on people who, for the most part, are doing the best they can and relying on God's grace. We want to help, not hurt, our people.

What are some ways you can stir up compassion in your heart? Look to the cross. A minister who loves God will naturally be moved to compassion as he sees the compassion of Jesus. Identify yourself with the weak and the vulnerable, for that is exactly what you are before God, apart from Christ. You will also want to spend time with the hurting. It's hard, if not impossible, to have compassion for those with whom you never, or rarely, interact. With respect to abortion, you might want to volunteer for a pro-life group or become a counselor at a crisis pregnancy center. And pray. Ask God to help you see the needy the way he sees them. Ask God to move your heart—to give you a holy discontentment at the continued practice of abortion.

---

34. Wilson, *Imaginations of the Heart*, 192.

Third, the prophetic preacher is *outraged*. If we would only see the massacre of unborn babies would we not cry out (Ezek 9:8)? Helpless babies whom God created and loves are being slaughtered. That is not an overstatement. It is not inflammatory rhetoric. It is plain fact. Abortion is terrible, and there's no place for ambivalence in one who would preach against it. We must be outraged at the systematic, legalized butchering of our children.

How do you cultivate this outrage? First, educate yourself. Watch a video of an abortion; look at photos of aborted fetuses; read pro-choice literature; and then see if your tears would not be mingled with anger.[35] In your anger, do not sin, but go to your knees and repent (Eph 4:26). Then ask God to complete your resolve and transform your outrage into a prophetic word for your people. And pray. Pray for a right sense of God's anger at sin and particularly at abortion; a sense of his wrath that compels you to preach against it, but restrains you from the violence and terror of those who kill abortion doctors. There is an anger that doesn't lead to sin. Ask God for that.

Fourth, the prophetic preacher is *wise*. I believe abortion is murder, but screaming it at people from a busy downtown intersection may not be the wisest thing to do. We need wisdom in preaching against abortion. We need to recognize the different kinds of people who hear us preach—some will be pro-life, some will be pro-choice, and some will be on the fence—and we need wisdom in communicating to all.

If you would increase in wisdom, get to know Jesus better. He was the wisest man to ever walk the earth. Get to know him better and you will learn and know what he would do, and you will act in a manner that pleases him. The chief way to be wise is to know Wisdom personified. Also, seek the counsel of other wise and mature Christians. If you've never preached against abortion you will especially want to find others who are involved in pro-life work and learn from them. And pray. "If any of you lacks wisdom," James says, "let him ask God, who gives generously to all without reproach, and it will be given him" (Jas 1:5). So, pray for wisdom.

35. Media theorist Marshall McLuhan proposed the use of actual abortion video footage on television as a way to show people what abortion really is. "When asked if footage would unfairly bias viewers, McLuhan replied, 'These films don't have to have any pro or con slant, if they are permitted to show the actual process'" (Molinaro, *Letters*, 503; quoted on the FAQ page of the Canadian Centre for Bio-Ethical Reform web site).

Finally, the prophetic preacher is *courageous*. We "must be more committed to courage than [we] are to comfort and complacency."[36] C. S. Lewis writes, "Courage is not simply one of the virtues but the form of every virtue at the testing point, which means at the point of highest reality. A chastity or honesty or mercy which yields to danger will be chaste or honest or merciful only on conditions. Pilate was merciful till it became risky."[37] History is filled with stories of men and women who risked, and even gave, their lives for the sake of God, gospel, and needy. The finest example is Jesus. Looking to his courage in the garden at Gethsemane and upon the cross of Calvary is the chief way to be made more courageous. What are you afraid of that he didn't already die for? He is with you, so take courage (Acts 23:11).

How else might we find courage? By now, if not sooner, you may have noticed a common refrain: pray. Pray with the hymn writer:

> Give me strength to do with ready heart and willing,
> whatever you command, my calling here fulfilling—
> to do it when I ought, with all my strength; and bless
> whatever I have wrought, for you must give success.
> When dangers gather round, oh, keep me calm and fearless;
> help me to bear the cross when life seems dark and cheerless;
> help me, as you have taught, to love both great and small,
> and, by your Spirit's might, to live at peace with all.[38]

CONCLUSION

One homiletician has said, "If a good case can be made for the place of justice in the gospel mission of the church, we will have made the case that it should be woven tightly into the fabric of Christian preaching."[39] He's right. And in light of our responsibilities as preachers, not to preach against abortion—the greatest social evil of our day—is nothing short of sin. We must address it from our pulpits.

---

36. White, "Call to Moral Leadership," 183.
37. Lewis, *Screwtape Letters*, 137–38.
38. Heermann, "O God, My Faithful God," 602.
39. Childs Jr., *Preaching Justice*, x.

5

Abortion and the Congregation

If you care about the slaughter of the innocent, then for God's sake, speak up. Speak to your family. Speak to your neighbor. Speak to your friend. Speak to your doctor. Speak to your minister. Speak to your congressman. Let your voice be heard in a chorus of protest. Yours is only one voice, but it is a voice. Use it.

—R. C. Sproul

Knowing what your congregation thinks and feels about abortion is critical to preaching effectively against it. You need to know who's listening to you so that you can adjust your message accordingly. Preaching at a pro-life rally will be different than preaching at your home church on a Sunday morning. Preaching against abortion to a group of teens at a Christian high school will be different than preaching to women who've had abortions. To be an effective preacher you need to exegete Scripture *and* your audience. This latter task is sometimes called *congregational analysis*, and effective preachers do this well. This means, at the very least, knowing about your congregation. How old are your people? Are most of them teens? Young adults? Empty nesters? What's their relationship status? Are they single or married? Do they have children? How much formal education do they have? Are they high school graduates? Do they have university degrees? What's their ethnic background? Do you have a large immigrant population? Do they come from countries where abortion is illegal? Or perhaps where abortions are commonplace—where the number of children a family is allowed to have is regulated by the state? Having a handle on congregational ethnography is helpful and will inform your preaching. This knowledge can help you with sermon phrasing and language, making applications, and emphasizing specific teaching points.

THE SIX LISTENERS

When it comes to preaching on abortion, it's helpful to remember that there are, essentially, six different kinds of listeners in your church.

Pro-life Christian	Pro-life non-Christian
Pro-choice Christian	Pro-choice non-Christian
Undecided Christian	Undecided non-Christian

Among both Christians and non-Christians are those who oppose abortion, those who favor abortion choice, and those who are undecided. When we preach against abortion, we need to speak to each of these six groups or risk unnecessarily alienating or offending a significant number of those in our churches. Knowing about our congregations means first, knowing that we need to address each of these groups a little differently, and second, knowing how to do it.

Let's take a brief look at each of them and consider what sorts of emphases will and will not work.

Pro-life Christians

Ultimately, our goal is for each hearer to move into this category. We want all non-Christians to know and love the Lord Jesus Christ, and we want all who favor abortion choice to become passionately anti-abortion. The presence of pro-life Christians in our congregations reminds us that we need to emphasize action. It's not enough to leave our sermons at the level of intellectual argument. We must exhort our people to put hands and feet to their beliefs. Some will claim to be personally pro-life but not actually be involved in pro-life work to any extent. Challenge them with the words of Scripture. Plead with them to see Jesus not only risking his life, but losing it for the sake of vulnerable, needy, lost people. Call them, in light of the gospel message, to go, and do likewise.

Pro-choice Christians

These are people who have put their faith and hope in Jesus, but either don't believe abortion to be a sin or don't believe it's one worth opposing. They are more influenced by the prevailing cultural sentiment than by the inspired words of Scripture. In order to reach them, you need to challenge their belief that abortion isn't a sin. Take them to task and show them how their pro-choice views are incompatible with their Christian faith. Many think being pro-life is being anti-woman. You need to tell them that this isn't true; that, in fact, in some countries abortion is used to eliminate girl children. You need to enter into their non-biblical worldviews and confront them with the truth.

Undecided Christians

Like professing Christians who favor abortion choice, there will also be believers in your congregation who aren't sure whether or not abortion is a sin. Use every tool at your disposal to move these Christians off the fence. Tell them what science teaches us about the beginning of life. Tell them what the Bible affirms. Tell them how united the church has always been on the issue of abortion. Tell them earnestly, lovingly, courageously. Tell them as you weep for sadness that unborn babies are being killed even as you preach.

Pro-life non-Christians

Not everyone who opposes abortion is a Christian. Don't be surprised to find non-believers in your church who are equally angered and grieved that abortion continues to be legal and commonly practiced. Praise these folks for their pro-life position, but hold out the ultimate hope of the gospel to them. Show them that in Christianity we have a God who became an embryo and experienced every stage of human existence. Preach to lead them to Christ, knowing ultimately that it will take a work of the Holy Spirit to bring them to saving faith.

Pro-choice non-Christians

Abortion is unlike many other moral issues. With these other issues we need to tell non-Christians about their need for Christ before telling them how they ought to behave. We want people to be moral, but we don't want them to confuse Christianity for just another system of morality. But if abortion really is murder, we can hardly afford to wait for people to be converted before we tell them to oppose it. This doesn't mean our preaching should, or must, become moralizing. We have to be clear that all the right actions in the world can't save us—only Jesus can. We have to ground our opposition to abortion in the context of the gospel. But we should call non-Christians to pro-life work, even as they continue to investigate the claims of Jesus and Scripture.

Undecided non-Christians

As with abortion choice non-Christians, we need to tell non-believers who are undecided about abortion both the necessity of believing the gospel, and the urgency with which abortion needs to be opposed. This group will tend to be more receptive to your pro-life arguments than pro-choice non-Christians will, though they may be just as unreceptive to the gospel. As with undecided Christians, use every tool at your disposal. Remember to pray for them as you're preparing your sermon.

By dividing the congregation into these six groups, I'm not suggesting that you address them each one-by-one, but that you weave things each group needs to hear into the natural rhythm and flow of your sermon. With both Christians and non-Christians, anti-abortion individuals and abortion choice ones, we need "to avoid . . . sinking into moralism." We need to "explain to the congregation that God's commandments are not heavy, legalistic demands that are unmercifully laid upon us. Rather, they are God's gracious guidance of us in the new life that he has given us in Jesus Christ."[1]

Remember, too, that in each of these six groups will be women who have had abortions and men who have been complicit in them. Your preaching must speak both truth in love and hope in grace. Not all of them will agree that what they've done is sinful. But many will, and they may be hurting profoundly. Don't forget them.

KNOW WHAT INFLUENCES THEM

Beyond being aware of, and sensitive toward, the various members of our congregations, however, we also need to know what ideas are influencing our people. How do we begin to enter their "imaginative worlds?"[2] Here are a few suggestions.

First, *read what they're reading (and what they're not)*. What books are people in your church and community talking about? What maga-

---

1. Achtemeier, "Speaking the Unspeakable," 23.
2. This phrase comes from Tisdale, *Preaching as Local Theology*, 48.

zines are popular? What web sites are they visiting? Which blogs are most followed? Print media (both traditional and online) continues to exercise a significant degree of influence over its readers. Your preaching will benefit if you're in regular conversation with these sources.

It's not just abortion-specific content that you're looking for. You're trying to get a sense of the big ideas that are capturing people's attention. You're trying to discern the idols specific to your cultural context that are antithetical to a society where the lives of the unborn are valued.

But don't just read what your people are already reading, read what they aren't reading. Read broadly. Discover what's on the cutting edge in philosophy, sociology, anthropology, psychology, medicine, and ethics, each of which are areas of study that bear directly on abortion. Not only will your own intellectual life be stimulated, but if you can communicate what you're learning in a clear and applicable way to your congregation, their lives will be enriched as well.

Second, *listen to what they're listening to*. The familiar saying that Christians learn most of their theology from the songs they sing is oftentimes true. Typically, this line is used to urge worship leaders to carefully choose the music to be sung on Sunday mornings. But our people are listening to songs throughout the week and many—maybe most—of these songs offer a competing way of making sense of life. Love ballads, for instance, suggest that true happiness is found in a personally fulfilling romantic relationship. Angst-driven punk rock offers, instead, a nihilistic worldview. All of these songs threaten to confuse our people, if not convince them altogether, of an unbiblical way of life. Preachers who want to be in touch with their people should have at least some awareness of what they're listening to.[3]

Finally, *watch what they're watching*. Paying close attention to what your people are watching can yield significant returns. Famed director Norman Jewison once called films the literature of this generation. What he meant was that movies have supplanted the printed word as the primary culture shapers. I think Jewison is right. In addition to movies, though, choose some of the most important TV programs and consider carefully watching them.[4] Benjamin Schwarz, literary editor of

---

3. For an interesting study of abortion in the lyrics of a particular genre of music, see Koloze, "Abortion and Rap Music," 103–18.

4. When Curtis Chang was a staff worker with InterVarsity, he observed that "at the center of the culture stands cinema. Movies convey the stories of postmoderns in a way

The Atlantic, suggests a handful of television series, in particular, that have captured the minds of Americans over the last decade:

> For more than 10 years, the intricate, multiseason narrative TV drama has exercised a dominant cultural sway over well-educated, well-off adults. Just as urbanish professionals in the 1950s could be counted on to collectively coo and argue over the latest Salinger short story, so that set in the 2000s has been most intellectually, emotionally, and aesthetically engaged not by fiction, the theater, or the cinema but by *The Sopranos, Six Feet Under, The Wire, Deadwood, The Shield, Big Love* [and *Mad Men*].[5]

Pop culture doesn't simply reflect the sentiment of a people; it is a powerful engine, driving social change. So, watch what your people are watching.[6]

LEARNING TO DISCERN

I encourage you to engage critically with popular culture. Read attentively. Listen carefully. Watch with discerning eyes. Our church members are influenced—some profoundly so—by the things they see on the small and big screens. These shows and movies are created by human beings with distinct worldviews[7] and their understandings of reality are

---

no other medium does. When I sit down with a table of college students at Harvard and ask them about their views on some historical event or philosophical position, some will give me polite, considered replies, and others will mutely shrug their shoulders. But when I ask what are their favorite movies and why, their eyes light up and almost everyone has something to say.... Indeed, in our fractured and privatized society, viewing and talking about films together are some of the few public activities still thriving" (*Engaging Unbelief*, 157).

5. Schwarz, "Mad About *Mad Men*."

6. It's easy to go overboard, so be cautious. David Gordon, drawing on the work of media ecologists such as Marshall McLuhan and Neil Postman, sounds a timely warning in *Why Johnny Can't Preach*. See, also, Schultze, *Habits of the High-Tech Heart*.

7. James Sire defines worldview as "a commitment, a fundamental orientation of the heart, that can be expressed as a story or in a set of presuppositions (assumptions which may be true, partially true or entirely false) which we hold (consciously or subconsciously, consistently or inconsistently) about the basic constitution of reality, and that provides the foundation on which we live and move and have our being" (*Naming the Elephant*, 122). For more on worldviews, see the helpful book by Hiebert, *Transforming Worldviews*. A readable introductory essay is Strom, "What Is a Christian Worldview?" 13–34. For a helpful overview of how to recognize a movie's worldview, see Godawa, *Hollywood Worldviews*. See, also, Cargal, *Hearing a Film, Seeing a Sermon*, and Johnston, *Reel Spirituality*.

woven into the television programs and films they make, sometimes overtly, often more subtly. Bruce David Forbes defines popular culture with a helpful illustration:

> Most of us already have a rough idea from the very phrase itself, but some clarification might be helpful. Scholars in the field frequently distinguish between popular culture from both high (or elite) culture and folk culture. To employ suggestive examples from the realm of food: high culture is a gourmet meal, folk culture is grandma's casserole, and popular culture is a McDonald's hamburger.[8]

Popular culture wields tremendous culture-shaping power, and preachers do well to get into the habit and practice of dialoging with it. Forbes offers several suggestions on how we might do this:[9]

1. listening to the voices of popular culture, being challenged and/or inspired by them;
2. philosophically comparing and contrasting values between a religion and the general society represented by popular culture;
3. condemning and opposing the influence of popular culture;
4. viewing popular culture as an ally in promoting certain causes;
5. attempting to transform popular culture when it is not already an ally.

Brian Walsh and Richard Middleton note that faith commitments lie behind every worldview. They suggest asking four questions to determine a person's faith commitment. We can ask these same four questions of any cultural artifact:[10]

1. Who I am? Or, what is the nature, task and purpose of human beings?
2. What's wrong? Or, what is the nature of the world and universe I live in?
3. Where I am? Or, what is the basic problem or obstacle that keeps me from attaining fulfillment? In other words, how do I understand evil?

---

8. Forbes, "Introduction," 2.
9. The following list is taken verbatim from his essay, ibid., 16.
10. Walsh and Middleton, *Transforming Vision*, 35. The list is in their words.

4. The remedy? Or, how is it possible to overcome this hindrance to my fulfillment? In other words, how do I find salvation?

Just as every person has an answer to each of these questions, so, too, do all books, songs, television shows, and movies. Sometimes the answers to these questions will be explicit and hard to miss. Other times they will be far less obvious, buried deep in the fictional universe that has been created. The more you practice asking and answering these questions, the better you'll become at discerning the worldviews underlying the books you're reading, the songs you're listening to, and the TV shows and movies you're watching.

While we don't preach on artifacts of culture, we ought to be aware of what's influencing our people. We should have a sense of the different worldviews competing with the biblical vision we cast before our congregations each week. Engagement with pop culture isn't a waste of time when done wisely. While it may not be absolutely essential to getting at underlying worldviews, it is a valuable tool. And worldview discernment is critical. When you're preaching against abortion, it's imperative that you enter into the belief systems of your hearers. You need to understand how they see the world. As Christians we believe abortion is wrong because of theological convictions—because of a set of shared beliefs about the nature of God and humanity. But non-Christians simply don't share these beliefs. They have, in many cases, entirely different ones. Pop culture offers us a window into what some of these beliefs are, and that in turn helps us in better contextualizing our message.

What's more, when we do watch television shows or movies or read books or listen to songs that deal specifically with abortion, we're provided with case studies to contemplate on our own, or better, to discuss with friends and colleagues.[11] After seeing *Juno*, for instance, we might think about how to address a young, unmarried, pregnant high school student contemplating abortion. Or following a screening of *Knocked Up*, we might consider different options for preaching to young women or families who find themselves pregnant just as their careers are taking off. Pop culture artifacts like television programs and films open doors to worlds we might, otherwise, not think of entering.

But how do you know where to look? For important, culture shaping books, one of the best places to start is with the reviews published in

---

11. See Doehring's helpful chapter "Using Literature as Case Studies," 141–52.

periodicals like *Books and Culture* or the *Times Literary Supplement*. For an idea of the songs that are popular, turn on the radio. Find out what the most popular iTunes downloads are. Look at the Billboard music charts. For film reviews, your local paper will be a helpful resource, as will reviews in magazines like the *New Yorker*. During awards season, different film academies provide ready-made lists of the year's most important movies. But the absolute best place to go for ideas on what to read, listen to, and watch is your own people. Find out what books are on their nightstands. Ask them what songs are on their iPods. Solicit some movie recommendations. There's simply no substitute for personal contact, because as important as knowing *about* your congregation is, *knowing* your congregation is far more valuable.

KNOW YOUR CONGREGATION

What's the difference between knowing *about* your people and *knowing* them? It's possible to know a lot of information about people without actually knowing anyone at all. Reading what your people are reading, listening to what they're listening to, and watching what they're watching, though helpful, is still one significant degree of separation away from spending time with your congregation.

The only way to really know the people to whom and for whom you're preaching is to spend time with them. If you want to know their position on abortion—what they know and don't know, where their struggles are, what personal experiences they've had—you must make the effort to get to know them, generally, and inquire as to their views on abortion, specifically.

There are at least a couple of ways to do this. Perhaps most obviously, do what I suspect you already do. Spend one-on-one time with a diverse cross-section of people in your church. While these may not be moments to ask specific questions about abortion, they will be opportunities to learn how your people understand the world. Find out what dreams they have, what frightens them, where they find value and meaning in life. Ask them how you can pray for them. The answers to these questions will all have direct bearing on how you preach against abortion. They'll suggest idols to confront, beliefs to commend, and attitudes to correct.

In addition to meeting one-on-one with different members of your congregation, I also suggest forming a small group that will meet one afternoon with the specific goal of discussing each other's abortion views.[12] Tell prospective members about the group's purpose and what to expect. Ideally, the group will consist of anywhere from four to twelve individuals, both from within your local church and the wider community. This is enough for lively conversation, but not so many that some people don't have time, or are too intimidated, to share. Give each member an opportunity to share candidly. Don't correct or pass judgment. Instead, encourage honest questions and frank discussion. What you'll learn from this group will help you tremendously in focusing your sermons, ensuring that you address some of the most common objections that your people will likely have. It will also remind you to tend to their most pressing pastoral care needs.

CONCLUSION

Preaching that confronts abortion will only be effective if we have spent time considering our listeners and the different worldviews they bring with them into the pews. Every Sunday we're preaching to both Christians and non-Christians, and in both groups there will be those who are against abortion, those who are in favor of abortion choice, and those who are undecided. Preachers, let us labor in love, spending time and effort learning how to speak to each of these people, so that we may lead some to Christ and pro-life ministry.

---

12. John McClure articulates something approximating what I have in mind in *Roundtable Pulpit*. Though I wouldn't go as far as he does in advocating a completely collaborative homiletic in one's weekly preaching ministry, I do recommend this book for the practical suggestions he offers on how to host a roundtable group.

6

Abortion and Pop Culture

With great power comes great responsibility.

—UNCLE BEN PARKER

IN THIS CHAPTER I want to consider the abortion message that's being communicated to our congregations by some of today's most popular television shows. We saw in the last chapter that our people are greatly influenced by the media they consume and that it's well worth our time to be familiar with at least some of these influences. The three TV shows I've chosen to analyze in this chapter don't give us a comprehensive study of abortion on TV by any means, but they do offer a representative survey of the message being communicated as we enter the second decade of the new millennium.

HOUSE

Since its debut on network television in the fall of 2004, *House* has consistently been one of the highest-rated and critically acclaimed dramas in North America. The show centers on the titular character Dr. Gregory House (played by Hugh Laurie), whose brilliance as a diagnostician is matched only by his misanthropic disposition. Each episode is fairly straightforward. Typically, the principal storyline involves a case that other doctors haven't been able to solve. House and his team of doctors at the (fictional) Princeton-Plainsboro Teaching Hospital in New Jersey are then called in and, after a battery of tests (many of which skirt the boundaries of medical ethics) and mistaken diagnoses, House (often serendipitously) deduces what's wrong with the patient.

House hasn't steered clear of controversial issues during its first few seasons. Abortion has played a prominent role and features significantly in three episodes, which makes the series a particularly worthwhile one to examine.

In "Sports Medicine" (season 1, episode 12; February 22, 2005) Hank Wiggen (Scott Foley) is a star baseball pitcher who's used steroids in his past. Because of his drug use, his kidneys have failed, necessitating a transplant. When Hank is unable to get on the transplant list, his wife Lola (Meredith Monroe) decides to give him one of hers. While she's a match, she also discovers during the testing process that she's pregnant, making her unable to be a kidney donor.

After some soul searching, she announces her decision to have an abortion so she can give her husband one of her kidneys. Hank, however, is unhappy with this decision, particularly since they had been trying to conceive for some time. Hank and House's associate Dr. Eric Foreman (Omar Epps) have the following conversation where Hank's resistance is made known:[1]

> *Foreman:* [Your] heart looks good. We can schedule the transplant.
> *Hank:* No transplant. Lola's not going to have an abortion.
> *Foreman:* Actually, your wife just told me that she was making an appointment.
> *Hank:* Well, I don't care what she said.
> *Foreman:* I think you two need to discuss this further.
> *Hank:* We've been trying to get pregnant almost since we met.
> *Foreman:* Well, it's your wife's decision whether or not . . .
> *Hank [interrupting]:* She wants to trade a child for a kidney. That's murder. I'm not going to let her do that.

Hank's initial objection to his wife's decision is rooted in their longstanding desire to have a baby, but as the conversation proceeds, he equates abortion with murder. Interestingly, Foreman doesn't respond at that point. He doesn't interject and correct Hank. In the scene he simply looks down. The viewer doesn't know what he's feeling. Instead, the scene closes with Hank calling abortion murder, and we are left to ponder his claim.

In the next scene, another member of House's team, Dr. Allison Cameron (Jennifer Morrison), tries to better understand Lola's predicament:

---

1. All quotes from episodes discussed in this chapter are from my own transcriptions.

> *Cameron:* Would you give up a baby for someone you love?
> *House:* Please tell me you don't have to decide. . . . Depends. How long would they live?
> *Cameron:* This is a pragmatic question for you?
> *House:* Fifty years, no problem. Six months, I say, let 'em die. I've actually given this a lot of thought. My personal tipping point is seven years, eight months, and fourteen days.
> *Cameron:* I couldn't do it.
> *House:* You found religion.
> *Cameron:* Do you have to be religious to believe a fetus is a life?
> *House:* There seems to be a correlation.

For House, abortion isn't absolutely right or wrong. It depends. For Cameron, however, abortion is the taking of a life, and she says she wouldn't choose to have one even if it means saving someone she loves. It's worth noting at this point that this is perfectly in keeping with Cameron's character throughout the series. She's been described as "the moral center of the show,"[2] and if viewers pick up on this, they may agree with her. Note, too, that House sees the defining of a fetus as a life to be a religious decision. On the one hand, he's biologically wrong: the fetus is living so it most definitely is a life. (It's frightening that so intelligent a doctor could so badly err on so basic a matter.) On the other hand, however, he's couldn't be more right. Whether human life of any kind has value and is worth protecting is a philosophical and religious matter. Viewers are baldly confronted with this suggestion straight from House's mouth

Faced with the prospect of his wife having an abortion, Hank takes a drastic measure and tries to kill himself by ingesting a number of pills. The doctors are able to save him, and Hank eventually explains why he tried to commit suicide:

> I want that baby. Even if I'm gone, that's a piece of me and Lola. Breathing. Walking around town. Going to baseball games. If there's anymore transplant talk from you [House], Lola, or anybody else, I won't screw it up this time. I'll take myself out for good.

Hank makes it very clear that he would rather die than kill his child.[3] But neither his emotions nor his logic are convincing to his wife. She confronts House in a hospital hallway:

---

2. Kyle, "'You Care for Everybody," 135.

3. He also reveals one of his idols. His unborn child has become, in the words of cultural anthropologist Ernest Becker, an "immortality project." Hank is in search of

> *Lola:* You're treating him for Addison's and you don't think it's going to work.
> *House:* He tried to kill himself.
> *Lola:* I know. He's confused. We can have another baby. I can make him understand that. I'm having an abortion. We do the transplant.
> *House:* No.
> *Lola:* I can make decisions about my body.
> *House:* And he can make decisions about his. He doesn't want your kidney.
> *Lola:* So, he'll die?
> *House:* Probably.

Unlike Hank and Cameron, neither Lola nor House gives any real consideration to the life of the unborn baby. Lola rationalizes her decision to have an abortion by claiming they can have another one. While this is true for the majority of women who have abortions, in reality there may be complications from the procedure making it impossible to conceive in the future. Lola also appeals to her right to choose what to do with her body, an argument that goes unchallenged. House's failure to correct her at this point may suggest to viewers that this oft-uttered pro-choice line of reasoning is both scientifically and philosophically credible, which of course, it isn't. Notice, too, that House tells Lola not to have the abortion, not because the killing of unborn life is intrinsically wrong, but because it won't make any difference. Cameron is right. Abortion reduces to a matter of pragmatism for him.

In the end, the abortion decision is shelved. House deduces that Hank has been suffering from inadvertent cadmium poisoning, and is able to treat and cure him without having to procure a kidney transplant. But House's views on the issue are clear: abort if it makes your life easier. The question that remains is whether viewers see this as the opinion of a brilliant diagnostician or the sad, illogical ramblings of someone who shouldn't be trusted.

In "One Day, One Room" (season 3, episode 12; January 30, 2007) Eve (Katheryn Winnick) is a rape victim who discovers that she's preg-

---

"cosmic significance," and has invested that significance in his child. If his child lives, Hank believes that he, himself, will continue to exist, even if his body should die. In other words, he may only be pro-life in this specific instance—when his immortality project is threatened. See Becker, *Denial of Death*.

nant with the rapist's baby. House assumes she wants to terminate the pregnancy. Instead, he's surprised by her reaction:

> *House:* You want to keep the baby?
> *Eve:* Abortion is murder.
> *House:* True. It's a life. And you should end it.
> *Eve:* Every life is sacred.
> *House:* Talk to me. Don't quote me bumper stickers.
> *Eve:* It's true.
> *House:* It's meaningless.
> *Eve:* It means every life matters to God.
> *House:* Not to me, not to you. And judging by the number of natural disasters, not to God either.
> *Eve:* You're just being argumentative.
> *House:* Yeah. I do do that. What about Hitler? Was his life sacred to God? The father of your child? Is his life sacred to you?
> *Eve:* My child isn't Hitler.
> *House:* Either every life is sacred or . . .
> *Eve [interrupting]:* Stop it! I don't want to chat about philosophy.
> *House:* You're not killing your rape baby because of a philosophy.
> *Eve:* It's murder. I'm against it. You for it?
> *House:* Not as a general rule.
> *Eve:* Just for unborn children?
> *House:* Yes. The problem with exceptions to rules is the line-drawing. It might make sense to kill the [expletive] that did this to you, but then where do we draw the line? Which [expletive] do we get to kill? Which [explective] get to keep on being [expletive]? The nice thing about the abortion debate is we can quibble over trimesters, but ultimately there's a nice clean line: birth. Morally there's not a lot of difference; practically, huge.

What's startling about this conversation is House's agreement with Eve's declaration that abortion is murder. That's quite a progression from the House we met in "Sports Medicine." But for House, that isn't enough of an argument against abortion. (Is it enough for viewers, I wonder?) He accepts that there is no real moral difference between a child *in utero* and one who's *ex utero*. But, as in "Sports Medicine," the issue is nothing but one of pragmatism for him. That should sound disturbing to viewers. His agreeing with Eve that abortion is murder should stop them dead in their tracks.

Later, House and Eve continue their philosophically charged conversation as he tries to persuade her that her life will be better off if she aborts her baby:

> *House:* Either God doesn't exist or he's unimaginably cruel.
> *Eve:* I don't believe that.
> *House:* What do you believe? Why do you think this [rape and pregnancy] happened?
> *Eve:* I don't want to talk about it.
> *House:* Me neither. Too bad.
> *Eve:* You know, I don't think there was a reason.
> *House:* So God does exist, lets you get raped, needs you to keep your rape baby for no reason.
> *Eve:* Maybe he was challenging me.
> *House:* He hurts you to help you. Well, I guess it's better than because he hates you.
> *Eve:* You're trying to convince me there's no God. Why would you even say something like that?
> *House:* Because you're throwing your life away.
> *Eve:* I'm doing what I believe!
> *House:* What you believe doesn't make sense.
> *Eve:* This is not helping me.
> *House:* Then I can't help you. If you believe in eternity, then life is irrelevant. The same way that a bug is irrelevant in comparison to the universe.
> *Eve:* If you don't believe in eternity, then what you do here is irrelevant.
> *House:* Your actions here are all that matters.
> *Eve:* Then nothing matters. There's no ultimate consequences. I couldn't live like that.
> *House:* So, you need to think that the guy who did this to you is going to be punished?
> *Eve:* I need to know that it all means something. I need that comfort.
> *House:* Yeah. Are you feeling comfortable? You feeling good right now? You feeling warm inside?
> *Eve:* I was raped. What's your excuse?

House doesn't believe in God and, therefore, sees no possible reason for Eve to keep a child that he thinks will constantly remind her of being raped. He reminds us of something I've seen plenty of Christian pro-life activists forget. When we argue for the unborn child's right to life we do so presupposing that God exists and cares about the way we act. Many of the abortion choice proponents in your congregation won't share this presupposition, which means as a preacher you need to do basic apologetic work before moving on to making a case for the life of the unborn.

Following their exchange, House (in an extremely rare moment of self-disclosure and vulnerability), opens up to Eve, confessing that he was physically abused as a child. That, in turn, prompts Eve to reveal to House how she was raped. In the aftermath of this conversation, we learn later that Eve did, in fact, have an abortion. We don't know why she changed her mind. Presumably, House gained her trust and she decided to listen to his advice. There is a hint, however, that House has been at least somewhat unsettled by Eve's arguments. While he's playing foosball at the end of the episode with his colleague and best friend Dr. James Wilson (Robert Sean Leonard), Dr. Lisa Cuddy (Lisa Edelstein), the hospital administrator and House's boss, comes to thank him for the work he did with Eve:

> *Cuddy*: She's going to be okay.
> *House*: Yeah. It's that simple.
> *Cuddy*: She's talking about what happened. That's huge. You did good.
> *House*: And everyone will tell you that's what we gotta make her do. We gotta help, right? Except we can't. We drag out her story, tell each other that it'll help her heal and feel real good about ourselves. Maybe all we've done is make a girl cry.
> *Wilson*: Then why did you . . .
> *House [interrupting]*: Because I don't know.

We're not given an invitation into House's thoughts at this point. We don't know precisely what he's thinking. But he has been shaken by his conversations with Eve.

If House was beginning to change his mind on abortion, he comes full circle (or close to it) in the episode titled "Fetal Position" (season 3, episode 17; April 3, 2007). Emma Sloan (Anne Ramsay), a forty-two-year-old single woman, has finally become pregnant after two miscarriages and four failed attempts at *in vitro* fertilization. After she suffers a stroke, House and his team realize that something is wrong with her baby, and that whatever is wrong with her unborn child is also killing her. Throughout the episode, the question of whether the fetus is a person is played out, with arguments from both sides. At one point, House corrects Cuddy when she calls Emma's unborn child a baby. "Fetus," he says to her, despite having earlier called the child a baby, himself. Does the audience pick up on this inconsistency and see behind it a sign of the inconsistency of his pro-choice views? It's hard to say.

What's obvious, however, is that House is morally ambivalent. When Cameron calls him on his pro-choice views, for instance, House appeals to the fetus's inability to do grown-up activities as justification for abortion:

> *Cameron:* Semantics make you feel better? Pretend it's not a person?
> *House:* Can it play catch? Can it eat? Can it take pretty pictures?

Later, House rebukes Emma when she refuses to let him abort. "It's not a baby," he says, "it's a tumor." Clearly, he's overstating to make a point. Whatever is hurting her child *is* also killing her. But that doesn't make it any less a baby any more than it makes it a tumor. Cuddy, on the other hand, sees the child as a baby who deserves to live:

> *House:* The fetus is nothing more than a parasite at this point. Removing it is an instant cure.
> *Cuddy:* You're not going to get Emma to see it that way. She's probably already named the baby, read him books, had conversations with him.
> *House:* See, you get it. She'll listen to you.
> *Cuddy:* No.
> *House:* If you let this woman refuse to terminate, you're helping her commit suicide. As her doctor my recommendation is against suicide.
> *Cuddy:* If the baby had a doctor, I think she would recommend exhausting all possibilities before taking its life.
> *House:* Then she'd be an idiot.

Later, Cuddy removes any doubt about what she thinks: "He *is* a person," she says about Emma's baby. And as House does a 3-D ultrasound, we clearly see the baby's eyes, nose, mouth, and hands. The visual imagery—quite astounding to see on network television—is compelling evidence for the viewer.

In a final attempt to save both the mother and her child, the doctors perform exploratory open fetal surgery to discover what's wrong with the baby. During the surgery, one of the baby's hands reaches out and grasps House's finger.[4] He caresses it, and the viewer can see he's either

---

4. The scene has similarities to the real life case of Dr. Joseph Bruner and twenty-one-week-old fetus Samuel Alexander Armas. See the story behind the famous photo-

emotionally moved, intellectually confused, or both. Could this fetus really be a person? Although he breaks the emotional tension with a joke, we can see that this event is still on his mind at the end of the episode.

After the surgery, House tells Emma that it was a success, and that both she and her child are okay:

> *Emma:* So my kidney, liver, and lungs are all fine, just like that?
> *House:* Just like that.
> *Emma:* That's amazing.
> *House:* What's amazing is how blonde your baby's hair is.
> *Emma:* My baby?
> *House:* The thing in your belly that tried to kill you.
> *Emma:* You've never called him a baby before. [Technically she's wrong, although he had not called him a baby in front of her.]
> ... Hey, thank you.
> *House:* Don't thank me. I would've killed the kid.

House finally realizes the gravity of what's at stake and what he almost did in urging Emma to have an abortion. In fact, toward the end of the episode he refers to the child as a person, a "kid." The case seems to be closed, then. House hasn't come to belief in God, but he has seen powerful evidence with his own eyes that an unborn child isn't any less human simply because it hasn't yet been born. Have his views on abortion changed absolutely? It's impossible to know at this point. As of early 2011 the show's producers haven't aired another abortion-themed episode.

DEGRASSI: THE NEXT GENERATION

Degrassi: The Next Generation (*DTNG*) is a Canadian television series that's been on the air since 2001 and revolves around the lives of a number of high school students. The show was preceded by three other series: *The Kids of Degrassi Street* (1979–1986), *Degrassi Junior High* (1987–1989), and *Degrassi High* (1989–1991), and the current version features several returning characters from these earlier shows. *DTNG* has proven to be a critical and popular hit with audiences in both Canada and the United States.[5]

The *Degrassi* franchise has never been one to shy away from sensitive subjects, and in past incarnations has covered AIDS, homosexuality, eating disorders, and abortion. *DTNG* has continued this tradition. In

---

graph at www.michaelclancy.com/story.html.

5. See, for instance, Neihart, "DGrassi Is tha Best."

"Accidents Will Happen" (season 3, episodes 14 and 15; January 6, 2004, and February 9, 2004, in Canada; August 26, 2006, in the United States) high school freshman Manny Santos (Cassie Steele) discovers she's pregnant after having sex for the first time. She's afraid to tell her parents because of a past incident in her extended family when her unmarried, pregnant cousin was sent to live in a convent in the Philippines. In fact, her fear plays a prominent role throughout the two-episode story arc. She's afraid of her parents, afraid of the physical pain involved in giving birth, afraid of being ostracized by peers at her school, afraid that being a mother will wreck her life, and afraid that her figure will be ruined. These are all fears worth addressing from the pulpit, and confronting and assuaging with the gospel.

Despite these fears, Manny initially decides to keep the baby, and together with Craig (Jake Epstein), the baby's father, tries her hand at babysitting as a way of preparing for what awaits. When they find they're unable to change even the baby's diaper, they realize parenting is hard work and doubt their readiness.

At one point, Craig's friend Spinner (Shane Kippel) confronts him on his seemingly carefree attitude:

> *Spinner:* Dude, you got a girl pregnant and you're just walking around like, "La la la, gonna be a dad, no shlabooggle?"
> *Craig:* No, I'm not.
> *Spinner:* Where's your future, dude? I mean, no keg parties, no spring break in Florida?
> *Craig:* For once I want to do the right thing, you know?
> *Spinner:* But you don't have to keep the kid. There are other things you can do.

In Spinner's words we see what many teenagers see as the curse of teen pregnancy: no more partying, no more freedom, no more life for "me." Craig has a better sense of responsibility. He knows the right thing isn't abortion, but isn't willing to consider the alternatives to which Spinner alludes. He wants to be a father. Manny isn't as certain, however, and seeks the counsel of Spike (Amanda Stepto). Spike is the mother of Manny's best friend, Emma (Miriam McDonald), to whom she gave birth after becoming pregnant, herself, in junior high. (That story aired during the *Degrassi Junior High* run.) They share the following conversation:

Manny: I want to know what being a single mom is really like.
Spike: Maybe like juggling six things all at once? Plus, all six things are on fire and you're standing up, riding a bus. And you can't stop for at least twelve years.
Manny: It sounds horrible.
Spike: But you get sticky candy kisses, Christmas ornaments made out of toilet paper rolls.
Manny [sarcastically]: Great.
Spike: Lots of women raise kids on their own. But doing it at fourteen was extra hard. All my friends went off to college, university, Europe. But, I stayed home.
Manny: I want to study fashion. You know, maybe New York or Paris.
Spike: That sounds wonderful.
Manny: But Craig wants me to keep it.
Spike: And he's always going to be there? Ultimately, the responsibility is yours. So the decision is yours, no one else's.
Manny: You mean, I don't have to do this if I don't want to.
Spike [shaking her head, affirming Manny].

Spike, despite not choosing to have an abortion when she was Manny's age, tells Manny that she has every right to do what she thinks is best for her. Many of the teenagers who watch this show may see Spike as the epitome of reasonableness. After all, she chose to keep her baby and did a good job raising her, but at the same time, she understands how difficult being a single mother is. There's no romanticizing teen parenthood. She tells Manny the choice is entirely hers. How seemingly sensible. Spike is a pro-choice supporter's dream spokesperson. The truth is, telling Manny "the decision is yours, no one else's" is an incredibly misleading and irresponsible thing to say. Manny is clearly in no position to make any such decision, even if it were morally permissible for her to have this power. It's clear how immature she is. What's more, Spike's words apply just as much to a toddler as they do an unborn child. As a single mother, the responsibility in that former case would still be Manny's, but Spike certainly wouldn't suggest that Manny be allowed to decide whether or not to kill a two-year-old.

Eventually, Manny musters up the courage to tell her mother she's pregnant. "I can't be a mom yet!" she cries. What she really means, of course, is, "I don't want to be a mom yet." Manny's mother is both understanding and supportive, and even offers to take her to the abortion clinic. Where her father is in all this is anyone's guess. We can only conclude that the show's writers want us to see that, as a man, he has no say in her decision. In any case, Manny's subsequent conversation with Emma is revealing:

> *Manny:* My mom was so much better than I thought she'd be.
> *Emma:* What a huge relief.
> *Manny:* You're not kidding. I thought I was going to wet my pants before I told her, but then I just came out and she's even driving me.
> *Emma:* Where?
> *Manny:* She's driving me to the clinic. I'm getting an abortion.
> *Emma:* You can't.
> *Manny:* Look. I know you think it's wrong . . .
> *Emma [interrupting]:* And your child would, too!
> *Manny:* I'm just trying to do the right thing here. For me. You know, for everyone, I guess. I wouldn't want to give a baby some crappy life with a mom who isn't ready.
> *Emma:* Well at least it would have a life. What about adoption? There are agencies with great counselors.
> *Manny:* I know, but I can't go through giving birth. It's so terrifying. And then going to school huge and everybody knows about it?
> *Emma:* You can get through all that.
> *Manny:* I can't. I swear. I'm fourteen. Emma, please, please, you have to understand.

Emma is visibly upset with Manny's decision. Nevertheless, she rushes to Manny's defense when Manny tells Craig she's going to have an abortion:

> *Emma:* Craig!
> *Craig:* Emma, you butt out. What she's doing is wrong!
> *Emma:* I agree with you, okay? If she was just some stranger I would be furious with her. But she's my friend and it's her choice.
> *Craig:* But it's my baby.
> *Emma:* And Manny's body. What about her?

At first, Emma appears to be a staunch pro-life supporter, forcefully telling Manny she can't choose abortion, and suggesting adoption as an alternative. In the end, however, she resorts to one of the most common pro-choice refrains: it's Manny's body, therefore it's her choice. What could have been a wonderful opportunity for genuine dialogue, sadly, degenerates into just another pro-choice cliché.

The writers of this episode do deserve credit, however, for showing us just how self-centered Manny is. None of her abortion choice arguments has any moral or rational weight. An astute viewer should be able to pick this up. It's amazing how many times she justifies her decision to end her baby's life by appealing to what impact having a child would have on her. She's incredibly self-seeking. There is absolutely no indication that she feels any responsibility.

In the final scene of the episode, Manny and her mother are at the abortion clinic speaking with a counselor (Tricia Brioux):

> *Counselor:* Do you have any last questions?
> *Manny:* Um . . . is . . . will it hurt?
> *Counselor:* Maybe a little. Like the cramps you have when it's your period.
> *Mom:* And it's safe? She'll be okay?
> *Counselor:* As the consent form states, there is some risk of complication, but it's very low. About 3 percent. So, if you're ready.
> *Manny:* Um, how will I feel after?
> *Counselor:* Everybody feels differently. Lots of women cry a little. Many feel relieved. As long as you're sure of your decision, then . . .
> *Manny [interrupting]:* I'll be okay.

But Manny's conclusion is far from accurate. Never mind that a 3 percent complication rate is far from negligible and is simply glossed over. Never mind that the complications that do occur can be severe. Most, if not all, post-abortive women are certain of their decision at the time they make it. Those that I've counseled, however, come to deeply regret that decision after some time—some the moment after the abortion is finished, particularly if they see the dismembered body parts of their unborn child. All of these women I've spoken with continue to be haunted by their choice to abort their babies and wish they could go back and choose differently. The portrayal of abortion on *DTNG* is simply a reflection of what many in North America believe: abortion is a hard, even sad, decision for women to make, but it's their right to make it. While choosing to abort is emotionally distressing, it should not be illegal. That's the pro-choice message of *DTNG*.

LAW & ORDER

One of the most probing television depictions of abortion aired on *Law & Order*. "Dignity" (season 20, episode 5; October 23, 2009) was inspired by the real life killing of abortion doctor George Tiller, who was shot to death on May 31, 2009, while serving as an usher at his church. Tiller was one of only a small handful of American physicians who perform late-term abortions.

The episode begins with the murder of Dr. Walter Benning (Matthew Boston) as he's seated in the back of a church, worshiping with his wife. When the police detectives arrive on the scene, the first person interviewed by detectives Kevin Bernard (Anthony Anderson) and Cyrus Lupo (Jeremy Sisto) is the church's minister (Michael Hollick). They ask him if he saw the shooter:

> *Minister:* No, I'm sorry. My eyes were closed, and when I heard the shot I hit the floor. I don't have Dr. Benning's courage.
> *Lupo:* And what courage is that?
> *Minister:* Dr. Benning was an abortion provider who specialized in the toughest cases: third trimester. He was one of the few willing to risk his own safety.
> *Bernard:* A lot of Christians would consider what he did murder. Any of your members believe in an eye for an eye?
> *Minister:* Our church advocates tolerance. Benning's been coming to services here without incident for the last ten years.
> *Bernard:* A devout abortionist.
> *Minister:* Walter Benning believed he was doing the Lord's work. Prayed to the same God as the rest of us.

Not only was Benning a professing Christian, his own minister approves of the work he did, and is proud of the so-called tolerant, abortion-approving stance of his congregation. Evidently, not all Christians are pro-life "zealots," a term used by Benning's wife to describe the kind of people who opposed her husband.

It's not just the minister and the wife who have an opinion on the subject. After Black and Lupo interview a suspect in Benning's murder, they have the following exchange:

> *Lupo:* You know what, forget the abortion debate. You should need a permit to have kids.
> *Black:* In your world a kid hardly has a chance to be born.
> *Lupo:* Know what? About that, not to step on your freedom of speech or anything, but we're not here to get into arguments with witnesses.
> *Black:* I don't know, Lupes. That nurse at the clinic basically admitted that Benning was performing illegal abortions.

Abortion and Pop Culture 85

>   *Lupo:* That's not the crime we're investigating. And if you think forcing an eleven-year-old rape victim to give birth is okay, then you and I have nothing to talk about.
>   *Black:* You got it backwards, man. The horrible thing is the rape, not the bringing of a life into the world.
>   *Lupo:* All I know is an unwanted child already has two strikes against it.
>   *Black:* That unwanted child could change the world. Cure cancer. Be president.
>   *Lupo:* Yeah, or put his finger on the button and blow up the world.
>   *Black:* It's not for us to decide. I was born two months premature. My mother was unmarried, poor, seven months pregnant. She panicked. Threw herself down a flight of stairs.
>   *Lupo:* So I almost had another partner.
>   *Black:* That's all I'm saying.

Lupo would rather avoid the issue of abortion altogether, but Black will have none of it. He's personally invested in the debate because he was almost killed by his mother while still in her womb. By revealing this aspect of Black's back story, the show's writers put a different spin on abortion by getting viewers to think about the kind of people who aren't given a chance at life, and showing them one who did. The conversation also shows the futility and illogic of arguing against abortion by positing some hypothetical future achievement the unborn child may accomplish. This, as Lupo shows, isn't a good argument for pro-life preachers to make.

As the investigation proceeds, the evidence leads the detectives to interview Kevin Morton (Bill Sage), the father of a young woman named Blair, who was seeing Dr. Benning to procure an abortion:

>   *Morton:* Blair's baby was diagnosed with Ehlers-Danlos Syndrome. The skin is so delicate the slightest touch causes tearing and can be fatal without constant medical care.
>   *Black:* But you were willing to take on that responsibility. That's a big commitment.
>   *Morton:* Yeah. I told Blair I'd work three jobs if I had to. We'd find the money.
>   *Lupo:* Your daughter told us she didn't want the baby.
>   *Morton:* She should have made the decision earlier. She's twenty-eight-weeks. That's not a fetus, that's a child.

During this interview we learn that the father is a science teacher. His occupation lends more credibility to his statement that a twenty-eight-week-old fetus can't be semantically reduced to something other than a full-fledged human child. But his words also suggest a difference in value between first- and third-trimester prenatal babies; that at some point, a fetus ceases to be an ambiguous creature and becomes a human being.

The police eventually arrest Dr. Benning's killer, a radical pro-life advocate named Wayne Grogan. Grogan's defense is justification. His plan is to argue that he was protecting unborn lives when he killed Dr. Benning. The two prosecuting attorneys, Executive Assistant District Attorney (EADA) Michael Cutter (Linus Roache) and Assistant District Attorney (ADA) Connie Rubirosa (Alana De La Garza), convene to go over their strategy:

> *Rubirosa:* We didn't want this trial to be about abortion and now we have no choice.
> *Cutter:* Not only that, the judge is letting [the defense attorney] Jenkins hitch his defense to a sick baby.
> *Rubirosa:* Referring to this fetus as a baby isn't going to help matters.
> *Cutter:* An unborn child is a life and a soul to me. I can revert to PC in the courtroom because it's my job, but I'm not going to do it in my own office.

Cutter appears to value the unborn, but refuses to let this personal conviction affect his job or public life.

During the trial, the prosecution calls a board-certified OB/GYN (Mark Blum) to testify. He not only thinks abortion is reasonable, but "the only responsible medical choice" in instances where the child will require lifelong care. On cross-examination by defense attorney Roger Jenkins (Richard Thomas), however, the doctor's own fanaticism becomes evident:

> *Doctor:* The right to choice is absolute.
> *Jenkins:* Absolute? You would allow abortions up to the very moment of birth?
> *Doctor:* In cases of medical necessity, yes. The decision should involve only the mother and her doctor.
> *Jenkins:* You don't believe society has an interest in protecting life?
> *Doctor:* Life as defined by whom? Crackpots like your client?
> *Jenkins:* So, even though Blair Morton's son was viable, even though science might provide effective treatment for Ehlers-Danlos Syndrome, even a cure during the chid's lifetime, you would have ended his life?

> *Doctor:* I don't indulge in pie-in-the-sky thinking. As of today, the life that child will experience is compromised and without dignity.
> *Jenkins:* Dignity? As defined by you? Would you volunteer to abort Blair Morton's baby even now [with the baby due any day]?
> *Doctor:* If she asked me, yes, I would. Threats and intimidations won't keep us from providing abortions to the women who want them.
> *Jenkins:* What if the law says you can't?
> *Doctor:* Even if the politicians bow to the hypocrites and fools, it won't stop us.

The doctor's testimony shows viewers that there are, in the words of District Attorney (DA) Jack McCoy (Sam Waterston), "fanatics in both camps."

To bolster their case, the defense calls Lisa Barnett (Jessica Dickey) to testify. Barnett's child had been diagnosed with a fatal genetic disorder, but she chose to keep her baby:

> *Jenkins:* What did your doctor tell you about your pregnancy, Mrs. Barnett?
> *Barnett:* I was in my sixth month. He told me my baby had a genetic defect called Meckel-Gruber disease. She'd be born with a soft skull and undeveloped organs. My doctor told me her condition was incompatible with life. He recommended I have a late-term abortion.
> *Jenkins:* And did you?
> *Barnett:* No. I discussed it with my family, but I decided against it. I knew my baby would die soon after her birth, but I wanted her death to be natural. I wanted her to die with dignity.
> *Jenkins:* And what happened, Lisa?
> *Barnett:* My beautiful daughter, Amanda, was born on May 5th. I never experienced such a sense of happiness when they put her in my arms. She had blue eyes, curly brown hair. She wasn't a monster like the doctors warned me. Amanda looked just like a normal baby.
> *Jenkins [showing a photo to the jury of the woman with her husband, family, and baby]:* And what happened to Amanda?
> *Barnett:* Later that night one of the nurses woke me. She said it might be Amanda's time. When they brought her to me, Amanda was struggling to breathe. She didn't cry or seem like she was in pain. I looked in her eyes and I sang to her. I felt like she was comforted by my presence, like she could feel my love

> for her. And then she slipped away. My daughter was alive for twenty-one hours.
>
> *Jenkins:* At any time have you regretted not having an abortion?
>
> *Barnett:* Not for a second. My daughter spent most of her life peacefully in my arms. My husband and I felt honored we'd shared her life, happy that she had died with dignity. We mourned her death, and after everything we went through, we felt clean.

Throughout her testimony the camera shows the jury, the bailiff, and even ADA Rubirosa in tears. Soft, sentimental music plays in the background. Even those who support a woman's right to choose can't help but be moved by Lisa Barnett's moving description of her experience.[6] EADA Cutter, for one, isn't even sure that Grogan was wrong to kill Dr. Benning:

> *Cutter:* Substitute slavery for abortion. John Brown [the abolitionist] for Wayne Grogan. In its day *Roe v. Wade* conformed to what we knew then about human life and science. Contraception was limited. Most birth defects were untreatable. Thirty-five years later, birth defects can be corrected. Disabled children are protected by a bill of rights. Contraception of every kind is available.
>
> *McCoy:* Yet people who don't want to still get pregnant.
>
> *Cutter:* So, their rights should reign supreme? My God! Cats and dogs have more rights than the unborn. *Roe v. Wade* wasn't written in stone. It could stand another look.

Sadly, Cutter's statement about cats and dogs having more rights than the unborn isn't empty rhetoric. He's not overstating the truth. While he hints at his belief that violence may be necessary to effect change, this episode doesn't follow that thread. What the writers do show us, however, is ADA Rubirosa having a change of heart:

> *Rubirosa:* I grew up thinking *Roe v. Wade* was gospel and that a woman's right to privacy was inviolate. But after hearing that woman on the stand talk about her baby dying in her arms. . . . I don't know. I don't know where my privacy ends and another being's dignity begins.
>
> *Cutter:* You want moral clarity? How about just doing your job. Put the bad guys in jail.
>
> *Rubirosa:* I'm glad that it's so clear cut for you, Mike. Unfortunately, I can't leave my soul in the umbrella stand when I come in to work in the morning.

---

6. Strictly speaking, however, she was wrong. Her baby had been alive the entire time she was *in utero*, not merely twenty-one hours.

EADA Cutter's job is to prosecute criminals. Regardless of his personal views on abortion, he's able to separate his beliefs from his occupational duties. But ADA Rubirosa finds this more difficult. There's something about her soul that she feels is at stake in the trial.

In the end, the prosecutors win the case and the jury finds Grogan guilty. The episode concludes with DA McCoy lamenting, "I used to expect people to be consistent; that pro-lifers would oppose capital punishment; that champions of human rights would claim some for the unborn. I don't expect that anymore. It's a big, messy world." For *Law & Order* the way to clean up this mess is neither the solution of thoughtful pro-lifers nor that of pro-choicers. The way forward is something in between. Late-term abortions are wrong. When a baby is viable, when it's able to live on its own, abortion should not be allowed. Until that point, however, women ought to have the right to choose.

This position might appear to some as a reasonable compromise, but it's not a new proposal. Plenty of other so-called moderates have suggested it in the past, but neither side of the abortion debate has found it appealing. Those who advocate abortion choice don't think any restrictions can be tolerated, and fear opening the door to even tighter constraints. Meanwhile, although some anti-abortion proponents do (rightly, in my estimation) applaud any move to limit abortions, none think prohibiting late-term abortions alone goes far enough. Does the unborn baby only become a human being worth protecting when it's viable? How does one determine when viability occurs? And with ever-improving medical technology, babies are viable earlier than a generation ago. Are we really saying that the unborn are becoming human beings sooner in the twenty-first century than they did in the twentieth? There's too much inconsistency to simply agree to the proposal that *Law & Order* would have us accept.

CONCLUSION

According to Catholic philosopher Peter Kreeft, "The pro-choice media routinely characterize pro-lifers and their position, as unenlightened, unscientific, and irrational, dependent on rhetoric and religion (which they often confuse), on blind faith or feeling (which they also often confuse), on fear, fallacy, fantasy, or fanaticism."[7] Our brief survey of *House,*

---

7. Kreeft, *Three Approaches to Abortion*, 11.

Degrassi: The Next Generation, and *Law & Order* shows Kreeft's assessment to fall short in describing what we find on some of today's most popular television shows. In these shows, pro-lifers include doctors and lawyers. However, none of these programs goes so far as to condemn all abortions (the way we'd expect them to be universal in their denunciation of racism, for instance), and God remains noticeably absent. Instead, they suggest a tolerance, even acceptance, of abortion in at least some instances. This appears to be a thoroughly civilized view, but make no mistake, insofar as it is not the truth, it is dangerous, and preachers need to be aware of its prevalence.

PART THREE

How to Preach Against Abortion

7

Conception and Gestation

*The [abortion] law of our land is immoral and unjust.
That should be declared from tens of thousands of pulpits in America.*

—JOHN PIPER

IN HER INTRODUCTION TO *Birthing the Sermon*, Jana Childers suggests the benefit of thinking about preaching as "a mother who conceives and gives birth to faith."[1] The different stages in pregnancy and childbirth—in Childers' words, "conception and gestation, labor and delivery, nursing and feeding"—can be likened to the process of giving birth to a sermon. These next two chapters consider the practical question, *How do we actually preach on abortion*, and take their titles from this metaphor.

You feel the urgency to preach about abortion. You want to preach about it. Now, how do you do it? There are a number of questions that I am routinely asked when I talk to other pastors about the necessity of preaching on abortion. What I hope to do in these next two chapters is address some of these questions, along with some others I've personally wrestled with.

These chapters are structured as question-and-answer dialogues. Though the format is, in a sense, artificial, I think it best captures the spirit of one pastor having a conversation with another, which is how this material is best taught and caught. In this chapter I address some foundational questions regarding the task of preaching, in general, and preaching on abortion, in particular. In the next chapter, "Labor & Delivery," I respond to questions that you're likely to ask in your study as you labor to prepare your sermon. I also address matters pertaining

---

1. Childers, "Introduction," ix.

to the preaching event—that moment you deliver God's message to his people. My hope is that you will find some of the answers compelling and informative, and that they will help you better preach against abortion in your own congregation.

What am I trying to accomplish when I preach against abortion?

The goal when you preach against abortion is, in one sense, no different than the goal when you preach any sermon. What is that goal? Stanley Hauerwas says it's to "help us locate our lives, especially the incoherence of our lives, in God's story"; to show "how the unintelligibility of our lives can be made intelligible by the gospel."[2] Martyn Lloyd-Jones puts it like this:

> [The chief end of preaching] is to give men and women a sense of God and His presence. . . . I can forgive a man for a bad sermon, I can forgive the preacher almost anything if he gives me a sense of God, if he gives me the sense that, though he is inadequate himself, he is handling something which is very great and very glorious, if he gives me some dim glimpse of the majesty and the glory of God, the love of Christ my Saviour, and the magnificence of the Gospel.[3]

Preaching on any given Sunday should, as both Hauerwas and Lloyd-Jones suggest, help people situate the individual story of their lives within the meta-story of God acting in history through Jesus Christ to bring salvation and restoration to our fallen world.

Preaching against abortion aims at doing just this. We call people to acknowledge the sin of abortion, to confess and repent of their involvement in it, and urge them to do something to oppose it, all within the context of the gospel story. This means, at the very least, that we explain to our hearers how abortion is a product of sin; that it was because of sin that Jesus had to come into the world and die in the place of sinners; and that because of the new life we have in him, we can turn from our former selves and live anew, seeking to please and honor God.

So what comes first, converting people to Christ or urging them to do something with respect to abortion?

I understand the motive behind this question, but I think it's flawed. Lloyd-Jones (to whom I owe a great debt in my thinking on preaching) says, "If a

---

2. Hauerwas, *Cross-Shattered Church*, 16, 19.
3. Lloyd-Jones, *Preaching and Preachers*, 97–98.

man [sic] is not a Christian you cannot give him spiritual help.... [T]he first thing you have to do is to help him to become a Christian ... and it is only then that you can apply your spiritual teaching to the particular problem. If he is not a Christian it is idle for you to try to apply spiritual teaching."[4] At first glance, his words seem to suggest that we shouldn't bother with preaching against abortion if there are non-Christians present. We should, instead, aim to convert our hearers to Christ through our preaching. Only then should we talk about abortion. (In churches that maintain such an order, abortion may be only discussed, if at all, in smaller venues, such as certain Sunday school classes, or members' meetings.)

But I don't think this is what Lloyd-Jones is saying at all. Every day in this country, babies are being aborted by the hundreds, even thousands. These unborn children, as I've argued, ought to be treated as full-fledged members of the human community. Consider what you would do as a preacher, by way of comparison, if you knew that thousands of toddlers were being killed every day. You certainly wouldn't say, "Well, that's tragic, but let me first try to convince you to become a Christian and we'll deal with that down the road." You wouldn't ignore the situation at hand. You would tell people about the horror and urge them to do something about it.

But because you're a preacher of the Word of God you can't just use the pulpit to tell them about their moral obligation. Even as you're calling non-Christian listeners to rescue the unborn, you're telling them of their own need for rescuing. And you're showing them that this ultimate rescue mission was successfully accomplished by Christ. So, the question is unnecessarily pitting heart transformation and social action against one another.

WHY DO I NEED TO ADDRESS ABORTION SPECIFICALLY? IF I JUST PREACH THE GOSPEL AND PEOPLE'S LIVES GET CHANGED, WON'T THEY NECESSARILY COME TO SEE THAT ABORTION IS WRONG AND THEN DO SOMETHING ABOUT IT?

This view is overly optimistic. While it is certainly true that "authentic spiritual renewal inevitably results in social and cultural transformation,"[5] part of the process of spiritual renewal involves people learning about issues like abortion. There is so much noise in the world that many people

---

4. Lloyd-Jones, *Preaching and Preachers*, 39.

5. Lovelace, *Dynamics of Spiritual Life*, 358. See his chapter, "The Spiritual Roots of Christian Social Concern" (355–400).

in our congregations don't know what to believe when it comes to such ethical concerns. On the surface, a lot of the abortion choice arguments can seem compelling. If our people, even after having come to know Christ, are buying into the idea that they need to have material things or romantic relationships or financial success to have a worthwhile, meaningful life—and we know they do because we do, too—we shouldn't be surprised that they also buy into some of the pro-choice ideology. Even though our people may treasure Christ, there will always be some other competing idol for the throne of supremacy in their hearts. This is true of us preachers, as you know all too well. So, no, we can't simply ignore abortion from the pulpit and expect people to see it as a sin. Instead, we should make them aware of it. We need to identify our people's idols, particularly those idols that explain why abortion is so rampant.

But more to the point, we shouldn't separate the proclamation of the gospel from telling people about abortion. Proclaiming the gospel means we tell people about what Christ has done, why he did it, and how our lives can, and should, be different now that we live under his reign. Everything belongs to him, and so, when we tell people about abortion, all we're doing is saying the unborn belong to him, too.

CAN YOU ELABORATE ON THAT COMMENT ABOUT IDOLS? WHY IS IT IMPORTANT TO ADDRESS IDOLATRY WHEN PREACHING ON ABORTION?

I spoke with a young pro-choice advocate recently who told me she agreed with many of my arguments, and specifically that she knew life began at conception. She didn't disagree that the fetus is a human being. "But, in the end," she reasoned, "the rights of the mother are more important than the rights of her fetus. It's her body." Educating people can only get so far. If we want to end abortion in our country, we need to transform people's hearts. Education is necessary because some people aren't aware of the facts concerning abortion, but on its own, education is insufficient. Often, there's an implicit assumption that if you only have the right information, you'll inevitably make life-valuing decisions. Some will, and thus, such ministries are absolutely essential; but there are a number of people who, like the young woman I spoke with, know all the relevant scientific facts, but won't budge from their pro-choice stance because they're still serving underlying idols.[6]

---

6. There's something else implicit in the suggestion that giving people the facts about

WHAT ARE SOME OF THESE CULTURAL IDOLS THAT I NEED TO CONFRONT?

The exact idols you'll want to confront will be specific to your own congregation, but the main problem is we live as though God doesn't exist or isn't sovereign.[7] The truth of our fallen world can be seen in four broad idols: comfort, approval, control, and power.[8]

You see the idol of comfort affecting abortion decisions when you hear people say they aren't ready for the demands of parenthood. A baby will change their lifestyle, they argue, and the stress of caring for another human being is too much to take on. They value freedom from responsibility and obligation, and emphasize their so-called right to privacy—their right to do what they want without being judged by others.

The idol of approval is behind those who choose abortion because they're afraid of being rejected by a boyfriend or husband, or perhaps, a mother or father. Being loved and affirmed by a romantic partner or parent is so important to the pregnant woman that she's afraid that either disclosing or carrying on with her pregnancy will lead to the loss of that relationship. So she aborts.

---

abortion will cause them to choose life. It's presumed that women will not choose abortion because of the actual and potential consequences to their own health. My experience doesn't bear this out. The problem with this approach is that it's based on fear motivation and self-interest: "Don't have an abortion because of what it might, or will, do to you." It discounts the fact that other fears trump the fears associated with having an abortion. If a woman is more afraid that she'll lose a relationship if she doesn't abort than that she might be at higher risk of breast cancer if she does, she'll simply choose to have an abortion. Education-based initiatives can be effective, and they are needed, but in my view, more emphasis needs to be placed on educating people that the unborn are living human beings, and abortion is wrong because it's murder, not because of what it might do to the woman having the abortion.

7. In chapter 1 we discussed several reasons why women choose to have abortions. Behind each of these reasons, however, is the denial of the sovereign God of the gospel. The ultimate reason women have abortions, and the ultimate reason our society continues to approve of them, is the rejection of a God who is in absolute control of the world and of individual lives; a God who is deserving of our worship. A theology that denies God's sovereignty leads, inevitably (though sometimes only after several generations) to radical individualism. A soteriology that does not teach God's electing grace in predestination—in other words, that says we choose God and he only chooses those whom he knows will choose him—teaches the effective sovereignty of man. In such a system God suspends whatever milquetoast "sovereignty" he might have so as not to violate our free wills. We choose (or fail to choose) him because we are able to resist his grace. Our power to choose is inviolate, even by God.

8. For more on this, see Keller, "Preaching the Gospel," 100–108. See, also, Keller, *Counterfeit Gods*, and Powlison, "Idols of the Heart," 35–50.

Other women have made their ability to control the direction of their lives into an idol. They say with the poet, "I am the master of my fate: I am the captain of my soul." An unplanned pregnancy throws a wrench into their well-laid plans. There's too much uncertainty. They feel out of control, and the only thing they can control is the decision to abort. They don't believe (or don't live as though they believe) that God is sovereign and "that for those who love God all things work together for good, for those who are called according to his purpose" (Rom 8:28).

Still other women are controlled by the idol of power. They believe life only has meaning if they're successful and have influence over others. If, in their minds, a baby doesn't fit the equation for that kind of life—if they think instead, that they'll be humiliated or that their prospects at success (however they define that term) are diminished—they'll decide to end the life of their unborn child.

If you want to preach successfully against abortion, you need to be aware of these idols and know how to challenge and dismantle them. A general pattern to follow begins by orienting your listeners to their underlying heart idols, then disorienting them by showing them how impossible it is for these idols to give them what they really want, and then finally reorienting them to the only one, Jesus Christ, who can really satisfy their deepest longings and desires.[9] Let me give you an example of what I mean.

Suppose you decide to confront abortion indirectly by addressing sex before marriage. The first step is to discern the underlying idol that leads people to have premarital sex. In this case it's probably approval (though that's not necessarily always so). You've identified the idol. But to really dismantle it you need to bring the gospel to bear.

A simple way to proceed is to show people that this is what they're looking for: the approval or affection of a significant other. But, you say, when you make the approval of someone else into that thing which makes you feel like your life has value, you've turned their approval of you into an idol. You've made it into a functional god that you mistakenly think you need to have to be a person of worth. It's not wrong to want approval, but you're looking for it in the wrong place. Psychologist Gordon Neufeld argues that what each of us wants and needs most is intimacy:

---

9. These three terms—orient, disorient, and reorient—are suggested by Walter Brueggemann as a way to understand the different functions of various types of psalms. See his "Psalms," 3–32.

to be completely known and completely loved.[10] The gospel says God is the only one who knows you perfectly and loves you completely. It's his approval that you're looking for and need. When you make the approval of your boyfriend the ultimate thing in your life, you'll do anything to keep from losing it. But you don't need to fear losing God's approval if you put your faith in Christ. How do you get his approval? You can't earn it. You can only have certainty of it by seeing Jesus Christ on the cross, losing God's approval so that you never will. Receive him now, by faith.

Are there any features necessary in each and every Christian sermon on abortion?

Yes, I think so. When you preach a sermon specifically against abortion you'll want to name and weep over the sin, urge your people to confess, and call them to act.[11] And you want to ground your preaching in the gospel, which means that your sermons against abortion will always tell people the difference Jesus makes when it comes to this issue. Let me elaborate a bit on each of these aspects.

First, every sermon you preach against abortion has to be clear that abortion is a sin. It's not just something you find horrible. God, himself, is grieved and angered. The sermon is not your opinion. It is a prophetic message, by which I mean you're telling people the truth. You're telling them what the Bible and theology have to say about the issue. But, second, the sermon is also a priestly message, which means just telling people that abortion is a sin isn't sufficient. You need to tell your congregation, as hard as it is to do, that they all bear some degree of guilt when it comes to abortion. Not all of them will have had abortions or have encouraged someone else to have one, yet both by buying into the idols of our culture that make abortion acceptable and by failing to do enough to stop abortion, we're all culpable. But a priestly message means more than just declaring blame, it also means we hold out God's offer of forgiveness in Christ to all who are guilty. Finally, the sermon is also a kingly message, which means you have to call people to live in light of the fact that Jesus is the king who reigns; the one to whom all of life belongs.

10. Neufeld and Maté, *Hold on to Your Kids*.

11. This schema comes from Christine Smith, *Preaching as Weeping, Confession, and Resistance*. While her hermeneutic stance and view of Scripture is quite at odds with traditional evangelical orthodoxy, I find her threefold approach to preaching on evil to be quite helpful. Regrettably, she doesn't address abortion in her book.

While it's important that a sermon on abortion contain elements of each of these three perspectives—the prophetic, the priestly, and the kingly—you can do all of that and still miss the central message of the gospel. You can tell people that abortion is a sin; you can show them that they need to ask God for forgiveness; and you can exhort them to go out into the world and work to end abortion, and yet, not tell them what difference Jesus makes in all of this. You've done little more, in that case, than give a moving moral discourse.

It must be remembered that the primary subject of our preaching is always Jesus. When we preach against abortion, we're looking at the issue through the lenses of one who treasures him. A sermon is a sermon and not just an impassioned lecture on ethics if it lifts Christ up. Scottish preacher James Stewart puts it like this: "One thing at least is clear: we have no right in our preaching to waste time on side-issues and irrelevancies. In other words, if we are not determined that in every sermon Christ is to be preached, it were better that we should resign our commission forthwith and seek some other vocation."[12] When we preach against abortion, then, we must preach Christ and the difference he makes to how we think about pregnancy, children, parenthood, and the responsibility of the church. A good sermon against abortion will name it as sin, call people to repent, urge them to act, and ground everything in the good news of Jesus Christ.

I DON'T HAVE ANY PRACTICAL EXPERIENCE WITH ABORTION. I HAVEN'T DONE ANY POST-ABORTIVE COUNSELING AND DON'T KNOW OF ANYONE IN MY CONGREGATION WHO'S HAD AN ABORTION. DO YOU HAVE ANY SUGGESTIONS ON HOW I CAN BECOME MORE PERSONALLY ACQUAINTED WITH IT?

There are a number of ways you might try to feel the pain of abortion at a more personal level if you don't have any direct experience with it.

First, consider volunteering at a crisis pregnancy center or doing post-abortive counseling. You'll have the chance to speak with women

---

12. Stewart, *Heralds of God*, 61. Ortlund says, "To preach on any passage of the Bible . . . without relating the text at hand to Christ, is not merely an incomplete sermon but a failure to provide the key—often latent, sometimes explicit, always present—by which the biblical witness is to be expounded" ("Christocentrism," 319). It's beyond the scope of this book to venture further down this path. For more on the homiletical philosophy that undergirds my approach to preaching, see the representative works of Edmund Clowney, Graeme Goldsworthy, and Sidney Greidanus listed in the bibliography.

who have had abortions or who are considering them. Imagine life in their shoes. Learn about their life struggles; about what drives them; about their dreams and aspirations; about why they had or are considering having an abortion. This will make your preaching incredibly more balanced. It will make you far more sensitive to your listeners. Alternatively, interview people who serve in crisis pregnancy centers or volunteer as post-abortive or rape recovery counselors. Ask them to share their experiences and insights with you.

Second, watch a video of an actual abortion. Go online and watch *The Silent Scream* and see, firsthand, the unspeakable evil that's done each time an abortion is performed.[13] Your heart will break. See the unborn baby cry out in pain and watch as he's killed. This is not a video simulation. Some might complain that this is too graphic and hesitate to being exposed to such images. May I gently suggest that you lay these concerns aside? Yes, the images are horrible. But they are horrible precisely because of the gruesome barbarity of the actual act. Watch, weep, and be moved to preach.

IF VISUAL IMAGES ARE SO POWERFUL, SHOULD I USE THEM WHEN I PREACH ON ABORTION?

I urge caution when it comes to this. During the question-and-answer time after his plenary paper presentation at the 2008 annual meeting of the Evangelical Homiletics Society, David Wells discussed the use of means in preaching. He suggests asking two questions when deciding whether or not to use any sort of media technology: (1) what problem is it solving (that requires solving)? And (2) what problems does it create (if any)? Asking these questions seems, to me, to be wise counsel indeed.[14]

This is not to say, however, that having some sort of visual aid is out of the question. You might hold up a 3-D fetal model, for instance, or have one on display in your building's foyer or fellowship hall. You may even show a video of an actual abortion, though you'll want to warn your people ahead of time so they are prepared. Alternatively, you may want to simply reference a film like *The Silent Scream* and tell people that they can find it on the Internet. Use wisdom in deciding whether or not to employ visual images when you preach on abortion. As Wells says, "What's needed is prudential judgment: what is effective?"

---

13. You can watch *The Silent Scream* online at www.silentscream.org/video1.htm.
14. See, also, McLuhan and McLuhan, *Laws of Media*.

How often should I preach on abortion?

We need to distinguish between preaching specifically *against* abortion, and preaching that touches on abortion.

First, you can preach specifically against abortion. The goal in these sermons is, as we've said, to bring people to recognize the sin of abortion, to confess and repent of their involvement in it and lack of resistance against it, and to call them to act.

But, second, you can find ways to bring in abortion-specific teaching or application in a sermon not primarily designed to address the issue. If you're preaching on Genesis 1, for instance, you might spend some time articulating how the doctrine of the image of God informs our thinking on abortion. While the sermon isn't focused on abortion, simply saying something like, "All human life is made in God's image, from the smallest embryo to the oldest Alzheimer patient. God created them," is to address the issue of abortion, albeit indirectly.

This means you don't need to restrict preaching on abortion to a one-time-a-year occasion.

Can I preach a pro-life sermon without mentioning abortion at all?

Absolutely. In fact, if we really want to effect change in our culture with respect to the life of the unborn, we can't limit our preaching on abortion merely to sermons against it. While I've been arguing for the necessity of specifically addressing abortion, we need to be after cultural transformation if we want to make abortion both unimaginable and illegal. This means we need to routinely exhort people to get involved in culture-shaping professions like entertainment, journalism, law, medicine, and politics, and teach them how to work with Christian distinctiveness in their respective professions and so change the culture from the inside-out. Preaching that seeks to abolish abortion can't simply be reactive. Yes, we need to offer the forgiveness of Christ to those who've had abortions. Yes, we need to show people the horrible evil of abortion that's happening across our country. And, yes, we need to urge them to respond. But, a truly pro-life pulpit ministry means being both proactive and reactive. This is absolutely essential. We need to show our people the biblical mandate to do mercy. We need to encourage them to work to make communities safer, education more accessible, and housing and childcare more affordable. All of this is very much a part of pro-life work. All of this makes the world a place that increasingly resembles the kingdom of God; a world where men and women would never think of abortion as a legitimate choice; a world where we all "choose life" (Deut 30:19).

8

Labor and Delivery

> *Yours is the greatest of all vocations. You will stint no pains on labour to prepare for it. But do remember that there is nothing that can avail if the warmth of the Christ passion is lacking, nor any substitute for a heart that burns within you as He talks with you by the way.*
>
> —James Stewart

Now that we've addressed some of the general questions you might have about preaching on abortion, let's move on to consider specific matters related to the preparation and preaching of abortion sermons.

What are some texts I can preach from?

If you've decided to preach against abortion on a particular Sunday and are looking for a text of Scripture from which to preach, consider starting with Proverbs 24:10–12, a textual unit where the historical context is general enough so as to make for a natural connection to the contemporary abortion debate. The sixth commandment (Exod 20:13; Deut 5:17) is another text from which you can legitimately preach against abortion and certainly, I think, ought to do so.

I could go on and give more suggestions, but in fact, as you learn more about the shocking parallels that abortion has with sexism, racism, slavery, and genocide, the more you'll come to see that there is really no shortage of passages in the Bible that might be used as the foundation for a sermon against abortion. I know of no better example of what I mean than John Piper, who has preached more than twenty anti-abortion sermons during his tenure as pastor of Bethlehem Baptist Church. Among the Scripture texts he has used to preach against abortion are Genesis 3:1–13; Exodus 1:1–22; Ezra 8:21–23; Psalm 8:1–9; 106:32–48; Luke 1:24–45; 10:25–37; 23:32–38; Acts 4:13–22; Romans 12:9–11; Ephesians 5:1–16; Hebrews 10:32–35; James 1:26–27; 4:1–10; and 1 Peter 2:9–17, among several others.[1]

Piper is able to use these texts—some of which seem on the surface to have nothing to do with abortion—in ways faithful to Scripture, because he shows the relevance that the theology taught in these different passages has for our thinking on the life of the unborn. I encourage you to do likewise.

WHAT ARE SOME OF THESE THEOLOGICAL THEMES THAT I CAN LOOK FOR?

Let me give you ten:

1. *Life is a gift.* Richard Hays and others have observed that the language of rights in the abortion debate has obscured the biblical teaching that life is a gift God gives us, not a thing to which we have rights.[2] With respect to God, we have no right to life. Our lives belong to him and not ourselves (1 Cor 6:19). Life is a gift that he imparts—that we should be thankful for, rather than scornful of; that we should celebrate, rather than terminate.

2. *The purpose of life is to bring glory to God.* The Bible tells us that we were made to glorify God (1 Cor 10:31). When we consider abortion, we need to see that it does not honor him a whit. How does terminating the life of a fetus bring God glory? How is it pleasing to him? How does it exalt his name and make his love known to the world? It doesn't. Abortion is not a selfless act, it is a selfish one. It isn't done so that he will be glorified but that our lives will be made a little easier.

3. *"Whatever does not proceed from faith is sin"* (Rom 14:23). Paul turns our common understanding of sin-is-doing-bad-things on its head. Sin, says Paul, is anything that comes out of a distrustful heart. Framed in this way, we need to show that the person considering abortion isn't proceeding out of faith, and this, the Bible says, is sin. She needs to repent and be restored.

---

1. See Taylor, "'Abortion Is about God,'" 328–50.
2. See, also, Hauerwas, "Abortion," 603–22.

4. *Children are a blessing, not a curse.* The consistent, overwhelming testimony of Scripture is that children are a gift from God. Consider the words of the poet in Psalm 127:3–5:

> Behold, children are a heritage from the LORD,
>   the fruit of the womb a reward.
> Like arrows in the hand of a warrior
>   are the children of one's youth.
> Blessed is the man
>   who fills his quiver with them!
> He shall not be put to shame
>   when he speaks with his enemies in the gate.

The one with many children is called blessed. Jesus embraces this same attitude by loving and welcoming infants and children (Luke 18:15–16). We do well to remind our people that children are always a gift from God to be cherished. We are to be thankful.[3]

5. *Parents have a responsibility to their children.* This should go without saying, shouldn't it? Paul takes for granted that parents have a responsibility to their kids when he compares his pastoral leadership over the Corinthian church to a parent's leadership of his child (2 Cor 12:14). One way of moving forward in preaching against abortion is to stress a father and mother's responsibility to their unborn baby, as opposed to a woman's so-called right to choose.

6. *The Christian community is called to imitate Christ by bearing each other's burdens.* While children aren't burdens, the task of raising them can become burdensome to even the most loving parents. This is particularly the case for poor, single women with few resources and little or no support system. It's equally true for parents with multiple children. The church needs to be responsible for bearing one another's burdens (Gal 6:2).[4] When we do this, we point to the ultimate burden bearing that Jesus accomplished when he bore our sins on the cross.

---

3. Pregnancy is a sign of hope—a tangible expression that God hasn't abandoned us. See Bunge et al., eds., *Child in the Bible*. For an expression of this in a different literary genre, see James, *Children of Men*.

4. See, also, McLuhan, "Private Individual vs. Global Village," 245–48.

7. *Human beings, including unborn human beings, are made in God's image.* Human beings are valuable because we're created in the image of God (Gen 1:26–27). Conception requires his creative, sovereign act. Other animals are called "living souls" (*nephesh hayah*, Gen 1:24), but only human beings bear God's image. It's this fact that makes murder such a deplorable and heinous offense (Gen 9:6).[5]

8. *God has a special place in his heart for those on the margins of society.* Throughout Scripture we read of God's love for the widow and the orphan and those on the outside looking in (Deut 10:18; Ps 68:5). God's love enfolds them all. He is concerned especially with their welfare. Certainly, the unborn are among the most vulnerable in our society. God loves them immeasurably and so must we.

9. *The necessity of neighbor love.* God's love for all people obliges us to show love to them. While it's true that we have no right to life with respect to God, we do have a right to live with respect to one another.[6] Abortion fails to afford this right to the unborn, so we must plead their case and defend their right to life. That's an unavoidable implication of the biblical command to love our neighbor.

10. *In the Incarnation, Jesus identified with humanity, including the unborn.* It's easy to forget that Jesus didn't come to earth as a fully formed man or even as a little baby wrapped in swaddling clothes. He became human at the moment of his conception by the Holy Spirit. He was a human embryo nine months before he breathed his first breath. So, he identified not only with the poor and the oppressed, but also with the unborn. And he sanctified the whole of life from its inception to its end.[7]

There's certainly much more that the Bible has to say about the contemporary abortion debate, but these ten truths give us a solid foundation upon which to continue building.

---

5. For more on the image of God, see Motyer, *Look to the Rock*, 66–79.

6. Nicholas Wolterstorff makes precisely this case in *Justice*. He defines rights as "normative social relationships; sociality is built into the essence of rights. A right is a right with regard to someone" (4).

7. The implications of the Incarnation for abortion have yet to be fully explored. Some helpful treatments include Crisp, *God Incarnate*, and Saward, *Redeemer in the Womb*. See, also, Jones, *Soul of the Embryo*, and Olsen, "More Important Than Christmas?"

DO YOU HAVE ANY SUGGESTIONS FOR THE KINDS OF SERIES I MIGHT PREACH?

One of the things we've done at my church is to preach a series on the relevance of the gospel to how we think about and act on the most pressing ethical issues of our day. During this series we asked, "What course of action or behavior is consistent with the gospel"[8] when it comes to poverty, racism, gambling, pornography, divorce, homosexuality, suicide and euthanasia, the environment, and abortion, along with several other issues?[9] You might want to try something similar in your congregation.

A series that approaches abortion from a more indirect perspective might examine the biblical sex ethic, and explore what the gospel has to tell us about God's gift of sex. We've already noted that five in six women who have abortions aren't married. In other words, most of the women who have abortions are having sex outside of marriage. If couples simply waited until they were married to have sex, we would rightly expect the number of abortions to fall drastically. A short series on sex, singleness, marriage, the roles of husbands and wives, and the duties of parents to children would aim to show people how to bring this area of their lives into line with the gospel, and in so doing, actively address the problem of abortion.[10]

In general, however, I think it's best to proceed organically when it comes to planning series of this kind. What I have in mind is something very much like what Martyn Lloyd-Jones encourages in *Preaching and Preachers*.[11] During the course of your everyday Bible reading (that is, your personal devotional reading and not your reading in preparation for the coming Sunday) keep a notebook (or word processing program) handy and when something in the Bible strikes you, jot it down. Lloyd-Jones suggests that right then and there you make "a skeleton of a sermon."[12] If you do this regularly, "you will soon find that you have accumulated a little pile of skeletons—skeletons of sermons."[13] This is

---

8. This phrasing is from Goldsworthy, *Preaching the Whole Bible*, 96.

9. This series was inspired by Kaiser, *What Does the Lord Require?*

10. Two of the best recent resources I've seen on this topic are Hollinger, *Meaning of Sex*, and Piper and Taylor, eds., *Sex and Christ*. See, also, Adam, "Strategies for Sex Education," 80–88.

11. Lloyd-Jones, *Preaching and Preachers*, 171–74.

12. Ibid., 173.

13. Ibid., 174.

the most natural way to develop a sermon series, particularly one that doesn't treat a particular book or section of a book of the Bible. Lloyd-Jones shares a short anecdote about the practical wisdom of such a method: "I remember once that, looking through my pile of skeletons just before leaving for my summer vacation, I happened to notice that there were ten skeletons bearing on the same theme. I there and then arranged them in order and so knew that I had a series of ten consecutive sermons ready for my return."[14]

I commend this system of Bible reading to you. I also suggest you take one year and read through the Bible, looking intentionally for anything that seems to you to have bearing on the abortion issue. Buy an inexpensive Bible and mark or highlight texts that seem to have particular relevance. Keep a record of these passages and your thoughts on them.

Are there any particularly important times of the year that I should make it a point to preach on abortion?

There's never a bad time to highlight matters salient to the issue of abortion if the text you're preaching on suggests it. And there's never a bad time to apply the theological argument of a passage to our contemporary struggle against abortion if it's justified by your preaching text. But just as Christmas is a good time to preach on one of the gospel infancy narratives, so there are also some dates on the calendar that are particularly opportune times to challenge your congregation with what the Bible has to say about abortion.

In the United States, "Sanctity of Human Life Sunday" is the Sunday nearest January 22, the anniversary of *Roe v. Wade*. Many evangelical preachers have chosen to preach on abortion on this day. Observing a day like this each year helps ensure that we address this matter at least once every twelve months. It reminds our people that abortion is a national tragedy that demands action.[15]

Another date to circle on your calendar is the Sunday preceding or nearest March 25, the Feast of Annunciation. This is the day many in the Christian tradition celebrate the angel Gabriel's revelation to Mary that she would bear the messianic child (Luke 1:26–38). We celebrate Jesus' birth on December 25. Why don't more of us celebrate his Incarnation nine months earlier? It might be that as we begin to do this, more of our

---

14. Ibid.

15. For a description of a similar practice during the time of slavery and the slave trade, see Brown, "Strange Speech." See, also, Kachun, *Festivals of Freedom*.

people and more of our cities will recognize that life starts at conception and not birth.[16] Advent—specifically, the four Sundays immediately preceding Christmas—and Christmas, itself, are also times conducive to abortion sermons.

You might also consider a short series between Mother's Day and Father's Day that covers the biblical role and responsibility of parents; the blessing of children; the function of the community in the family of God; the gift of life; and the sovereignty and grace of God.

ARE THERE ANY SPECIFIC OBJECTIONS THAT I NEED TO ADDRESS IN A SERMON ON ABORTION?

Again, your interaction with people in your church and community will give you a better grasp on what objections you need to address from the pulpit. The important thing to remember is that you don't need to address each of these in every abortion sermon. In fact, you shouldn't address each objection. Instead, take one or two of them, articulate them, and then show how they're incompatible with real gospel faith. I will say that one significant objection to speak to is the mistaken notion that to be pro-life is to be anti-woman. Particularly if you're a male, there will be some (maybe many) women (and men) in your congregation who think you're in no place to tell them what to do. They'll think that being anti-abortion is synonymous with being a misogynist. You need to show them the flaws in this line of reasoning. As the authors of the blog *ProWomanProLife* say, "The idea that abortion is a woman's right was always just an opinion. There's no basis in law, in logic or in our constitution. And there's certainly no basis in early feminist thought."[17]

Another way to ensure that people's objections are heard is to incorporate a post-sermon question-and-answer time. If your congregation is anything like mine, these times will yield thoughtful questions—some you anticipated but didn't have time to bring up in your sermon, and some that just never crossed your mind. They will provide a great opportunity to elaborate on some of the things you said in your sermon.

---

16. For a similar reason I encourage people to call husbands and wives "parents" the moment they announce their pregnancy, while the baby is still *in utero*. We usually congratulate people after their baby has been born and refrain from calling them moms and dads (or grandmothers and grandfathers) until after the child's birth. This shouldn't be. We should recognize that just as the life of the baby begins at conception, so too does parenthood, and change our language accordingly.

17. ProWomanProLife, "The Story."

WHAT PITFALLS SHOULD I BE MINDFUL OF WHEN I PREACH ON ABORTION?

In 1 Thessalonians 5:14 Paul charges the recipients of his letter to "admonish the idle, encourage the fainthearted, help the weak, be patient with them all." In the spirit of that verse, let me give you three pitfalls to avoid.

Moralism. Admonish your congregation for the guilt they bear with respect to abortion, but admonish them not because they should know better, but because they aren't living "in step with the truth of the gospel" (Gal 2:14). If you don't present the gospel when you preach against abortion, at the very least you run the risk that your people will think being a Christian is simply about acting morally and being virtuous. Our ultimate aim as preachers isn't to change behaviors but to change hearts; that requires supernatural intervention. To be sure, we want people to change their actions—we want to end abortion—but we recognize that it will take nothing short of spiritual transformation to effect the broad social and cultural change we're praying for.

Condemnation. When we preach against abortion, we need to remember that there will be people in our congregations who've had them and are looking for hope. They're already feeling crushed by guilt and despair. And it's not just women but men, as well, who feel this burden.[18] We need to hold out Christ's offer of forgiveness and promise of pardon.[19] We must encourage those who are fainthearted.

At the same time, be careful not to demonize those who support abortion choice. For the most part, these are people who care about human rights but are tragically wrong in how they've gone about it. Confront them, but be wise, courteous, and respectful in how you do it.

---

18. For a poignant and insightful discussion of the guilt men often experience with abortion, see Condon and Hazard, *Fatherhood Aborted.*

19. However, this doesn't mean that feeling guilty is wrong. Don't be too hasty in trying to erase guilt altogether. We want people to feel guilty if they don't think they've done anything wrong. It's only by acknowledging their sin that they'll seek repentance. We should also question the idea that there's something wrong with feeling guilty. If men and women in your church start to see abortion as murder, and those who've had abortions see that they've murdered their own helpless, innocent children, guilt is inevitable. Even if they accept Christ's offer of forgiveness, they'll likely live with this guilt for the rest of their lives. The hope of the gospel isn't that this guilty conscience is somehow assuaged, but that God has imputed this guilt to Christ, and he will not ultimately make you pay for it.

Antinomianism. It may be surprising that you can preach against abortion yet not call people to go far enough. You need to exhort your congregation to confess, especially those who have had abortions.[20] You need to call all of them to act. Give practical suggestions on how those in your congregation can take up the cause of the unborn. Give them ideas on how they can apply the message of your sermon and help the weakest members of your community.

In all of your abortion preaching, be patient. We don't expect our world to change overnight. We don't think everyone in our churches will suddenly get involved in pro-life ministries after hearing one sermon. Keep to it. Persevere. Be patient with your people.

Are there any specific ways I can encourage my church to get involved?

The list of things you can encourage your congregation to do is limited only by your imagination. Recognize that not everyone will be called to the same level of involvement; but certainly, there are some things that everyone can do. Everyone can write to their local politicians and encourage them to defend the rights of the unborn. Everyone can write letters of encouragement to those who work in pro-life ministries. Everyone can routinely pray and fast as they anticipate the day when abortion will be no more. Therefore, call everyone to these things.

Urge others in your congregation to support pro-life groups, crisis pregnancy centers, post-abortive counseling centers, and rape recovery agencies, both with their prayers and their finances. Suggest participating in a march for life, demonstrating outside an abortion clinic, becoming a member of a local right-to-life group, doing counseling work, and participating in acts of civil disobedience.[21]

Tell people who've had abortions to confess to God and to consider sharing privately with you. They may even be able to share with the rest of the church during a testimony time. Confession has the capacity to transform these post-abortive women (and men) into great advocates

---

20. There may be some in your church who admit to having had an abortion, but refuse to acknowledge their sin. In this case, you may, eventually, need to administer church discipline. This is a sensitive area in the church today. Some helpful resources are Adams, *Handbook of Church Discipline*; Dever, *Nine Marks*, 167–94; and Schlossberg and Achtemeier, *Not My Own*, 91–104. The August 2005 issue of *Christianity Today* is also devoted to the subject of church discipline, and worth consulting.

21. On this last suggestion, see Belz, *Suffer the Little Children*.

for the rights of the unborn, though certainly, not every woman (or man) will be able to do this, given the deep wounds and trauma of their experience.

Finally, encourage adoption. Show people how our spiritual adoption into God's family should make us outspoken advocates and practitioners of physical adoption. Let's welcome other people's unwanted children into our households and faith communities.[22]

CONCLUSION

There's a quaint little statement, often uttered, that likens the church to a hospital for sinners. When it comes to abortion, this analogy is apt. Some enter our doors knowing they're sick and in need of spiritual surgery. Just as a good physician won't merely treat their symptoms but will diagnose their disease and deal with the real problem, so must we, preachers, get at the reason abortion is rampant in our culture. But just as there are hospital visitors who haven't a clue they're ill, others will come in to our churches not knowing they're sick at all. They won't know their spiritual deadness. They haven't a clue there's anything wrong with abortion. We need to tell them. We need to proclaim the gospel and seek to bring people's thinking and action into line with it when it comes to the killing of the unborn.

These last two chapters have offered some suggestions on how to do this under the titles "Conception and Gestation" and "Labor and Delivery." A third section, "Nursing and Feeding," which suggests and describes ways to mobilize your whole church for pro-life ministry is a natural next step, but outside the scope of this book. I pray someone will take me up on the challenge to write such a volume.[23]

In the final chapter I present two of my own pro-life sermons. I do this recognizing that when we separate the written word from the spoken word—when we consider the sermon outside the original preaching event; when we remove the sermon from the context in which it was originally preached and heard—something essential is lost. Still, there can be benefit derived even from reading a sermon. I offer these two sermons, then, as examples of my own, imperfect attempts to tell my people about the sin of abortion.

---

22. There's no better book on this than Moore, *Adopted for Life*.
23. As a starting point, I propose some very preliminary thoughts in Appendix A.

9

Two Sermons

THE DAY OF ADVERSITY

> ¹⁰*If you faint in the day of adversity,*
>   *your strength is small.*
> ¹¹*Rescue those who are being taken away to death;*
>   *hold back those who are stumbling to the slaughter.*
> ¹²*If you say, "Behold, we did not know this,"*
>   *does not he who weighs the heart perceive it?*
>   *Does not he who keeps watch over your soul know it,*
>   *and will he not repay man according to his work?*
>
> —Proverbs 24:10–12

Our text this morning tells us that we need to have courage in the day of adversity.[1] We can't faint. Our strength must not be small. We need to be courageous. Friends, we live in just such a day today. What do I mean?

Have you seen the movie *Juno*? It's about a high school student (named Juno) who finds out she's pregnant after having sex for the first time. There's a scene where Juno is outside a clinic, on her way in to

---

1. I've preached variations of this sermon on a few different occasions, first in my own congregation, Trinity Pacific Church, on April 26, 2009. I want to thank my good friend Ho-Ming Tsui for inviting me to preach a version of it to his congregation at Richmond Hill Christian Community Church, Toronto, ON. Both this sermon and the next were originally written for the ear, not the eye, and I've opted to retain them in their original form. These aren't transcriptions, which means during the actual preaching of these sermons I took extemporaneous liberties, omitting portions and adding sections. That's part of what happens in the preaching event. These two sermon manuscripts do not reflect those additions and deletions.

have an abortion, when she's confronted by a classmate named Su-Chin. Now, Su-Chin is not very attractive by our culture's standards. She's not good with the English language. She's not popular in school. You watch the film and you're supposed to laugh at her. But one thing she is, is courageous. Su-Chin is outside the abortion clinic because she's trying her best to convince people not to have an abortion. Here's what she says to Juno: "Your baby probably has a beating heart, you know? It can feel pain, and it has fingernails."

A beating heart.

Can feel pain.

Has fingernails.

In fact, between the third and fourth week of pregnancy, the baby's heart is already beating with her own blood. Arms and legs are also already forming by week four. In weeks nine and ten fingernails develop. And by week twelve, if not sooner, the baby can experience pain. Long before any of these milestones, however, the baby was conceived. And every single embryologist agrees that conception—when a sperm fertilizes an egg—is when human life begins. It's not on its way to becoming human life. It already is human life! When the sperm fertilizes the egg, all of the baby's genetic characteristics are determined. What color her eyes will be, or her hair. The embryo has a completely different DNA than either her father or mother. She is *not* a part of her mother's body, as some would have us believe.

Yet in Canada we kill one hundred thousand unborn babies every year. We kill them because it's easier than having to raise a child when we don't think we're ready. We kill them because we have sex before we're married and we don't dare become parents right now. Or we're afraid to tell our own parents; afraid of how they'll react. We kill them because we have other things we want to do with our lives. We kill them because we find out they have a genetic disorder like Down's syndrome, and think it's better that they die than live.

In fact, here in Ontario your provincial health care (funded by the taxes that all of us in this room pay) will cover the cost of your abortion at a hospital or a clinic, and you can find a licensed doctor willing to perform your abortion for you up to twenty-four weeks of pregnancy.[2]

Why? Because in Canada the unborn child isn't a legally recognized person deserving protection. Under section 223 of the *Criminal Code of*

---

2. National Abortion Federation, "Abortion Coverage by Region."

Canada a fetus is a "human being . . . when it has completely proceeded, in a living state, from the body of its mother."[3] Did you catch that? You aren't recognized as a human being in our country until you're born. Your entire body needs to be outside of your mom in order for you to be considered one.

So, in 1996 Brenda Drummond tried to abort her nine-month-old unborn baby, just days from its birth, by putting a pellet gun into her vagina and shooting her baby in the head. They tried to charge her with attempted murder but the charges had to be dropped because a fetus isn't a human being according to Canadian law. Or consider the case of two midwives charged with criminal negligence causing death and bodily harm in a botched delivery (*R. v. Sullivan*). The midwives were found not guilty because, again, a fetus isn't a person.

What's really bizarre is that a fetus is a person in some countries, not a person in others, and might be a person depending on how old it is in still others. But logically we know this can't be true. A Canadian fetus isn't different in value than a Chinese fetus or an Irish fetus. The fact of the matter is that an unborn baby in Canada has no legal right to life until she's born—until every part of her body is outside of her mother's.

So, what are we supposed to do about this?

Why Must We Oppose Abortion?

Proverbs 24:11 says our obligation is to "rescue those who are being taken away to death; [to] hold back those who are stumbling to the slaughter." The reason for this procession to the grave isn't given. The context is broad and left ambiguous, I think, on purpose. *Anytime* someone needs a voice to speak for them, *anytime* someone is marginalized, *anytime* someone is being oppressed, it's our responsibility to intercede on their behalf.

So, why should we oppose abortion? Why should we try to rescue the unborn? For one, simply because they're being taken away to death. They're being slaughtered! The government isn't doing anything about it. The legal system doesn't protect them. So, if not us, who?

But second, we should oppose abortion for the same reason we oppose any injustice. Because people made in God's image are being de-

---

3. Department of Justice Canada, "Criminal Code of Canada."

stroyed. The Bible says that God made human beings in his image. That's where all human rights are ultimately grounded.

Why do we say it's wrong for a woman to be raped or a child to be killed? Because human beings have an inherent worth, an intrinsic value. But where does this value come from? At the end of the day if you say you believe human beings have rights—that a human being has worth and value—you're grounding that in what the Bible says is our bearing the image of God. Friends, when a child is conceived, God's creative act has begun. It's not our right to destroy that act. And it absolutely is our responsibility to protect that child.

If we're not made in God's image, there's nothing wrong with rape and murder. If we're all the products of random evolutionary forces, and life is just a matter of survival of the fittest, why shouldn't men rape women? Why shouldn't we kill those who are weaker than us? We have no objective basis for saying anything is right or wrong. But the Bible says we're made in God's image, and that's why murder is condemned, because we're killing someone made in his image. And that's exactly what happens in abortion. We murder someone made in the image of God.

The unborn need us to speak out for them. And we have to. When we don't, it's a leap to suppose that God will hear our prayers and accept our worship. In fact, the Bible is filled with examples of God rejecting his people's praise and sacrifice when their words and offerings aren't accompanied by tangible concern for justice and mercy (Isa 1:10–18; Amos 5:21–24). Voiceless, powerless babies are being killed, one hundred thousand a year in our country. God calls us to act. We have to.

Addressing Objections

Now, some of you might have some objections at this point. And our text in Proverbs anticipates some protest in verse 12: "If you say, 'Behold, we did not know this,' does not he who weighs the heart perceive it? Does not he who keeps watch over your soul know it, and will he not repay man according to his work?" According to Old Testament scholar Bruce Waltke, the picture here is of a person who "locates himself within a whole community that is claiming ignorance to escape their culpability."[4] But the Proverbs writer says these excuses won't fly with God. We can't say to him that we simply didn't know. That's not going to cut it. Ellen

---

4. Waltke, *Book of Proverbs*, 277.

Davis, a commentator on Proverbs, rightly draws a connection between this passage and the Holocaust. She says "modern readers cannot fail to see here haunting reflections of recent history: the Nazi Holocaust, when both public officials and private citizens of Europe and North America chose 'not to know' about the destruction of the Jews until it was too late."[5] In much the same way, we can't make this sort of excuse when it comes to abortion. We need to do something.

But before we consider some ideas of what we can do, some of you do have some real questions. You're not trying to make excuses. It's just that you've heard lots of pro-choice arguments on TV, in school, from friends, and you're not sure what to do with them. Let me address some of the most common objections that I've heard and that you've probably heard, too.

First, some people say we can't know for sure when a fetus is a human life. We know from biology that life begins at conception, but does life mean this is a person? A real human being? Here's how I'd respond. Even if we grant this objection, there's something called the doctrine of carefulness that says we should err on the side of caution. If it's possible that this tiny fetus is a human being, we should be careful and protect it. Just as we wouldn't throw a live grenade into a room without knowing whether there's anyone inside it, we shouldn't abort if we're not 100 percent sure the unborn child is not a human being.

Second, you might hear some people say that since the baby is inside a woman's body, she, and she alone, should have the right to decide and do what she wants. But the truth is, the fetus isn't a part of the woman's body. It's its own body. A fetus has a body. It may be just a single cell at the beginning of its life, or a small cluster of cells a few weeks later, but that is still a body. After all, your grown up body is really just a whole bunch of cells. More importantly, the Bible tells us that your life is *not* your own to do with as you please. You were made by God and for God. The Apostle Paul says, "Your body is a temple of the Holy Spirit within you. . . . You are not your own, for you were bought with a price. So glorify God in your body" (1 Cor 6:19–20). Friends, abortion does not glorify God. Abortion says, "I'm God! I get to decide." That's tragic. We can't bear that responsibility.

A third objection says we shouldn't legislate our morality. We might believe abortion to be wrong, but we shouldn't tell other people

---

5. Davis, *Proverbs*, 128.

what they can or can't do. But that's exactly the point of the legal system. We legislate morality all the time—and we should—when we say you can't murder, rape, or abuse another person. If someone says, "I believe certain ethnicities are inferior and ought to be eliminated," we rightly respond by saying, "You're wrong. You can't do that. Your morality is flawed." To say we shouldn't legislate morality with respect to abortion is illogical. That's exactly what we need to do.

A fourth objection says it's better to abort than to bring an unwanted baby into the world. But if the unborn child is a human life, this argument falls apart. Would we say the same thing of an unwanted two-year-old? If my wife and I were to decide that we don't want our kids anymore, does that give us the right to kill them? Of course not. Just because a parent doesn't want to be burdened by a baby doesn't give them the right to end that baby's life. And I want to say to those of you here, being a parent is really hard work. There are lots of burdens involved. But your child is not a burden. She's a blessing. She's a great blessing. In fact, all throughout the Bible, children are only ever described as gifts from God. Not hardships.

There are lots of other objections, of course, but those are four of the most prominent ones. You may have other questions. Don't leave them unasked. Come find me after service and I'll be happy to speak with you.

How Must We Respond?

Now in light of all we've said, how must we respond to abortion? First, we need to repent. If you've had an abortion or encouraged someone to have an abortion, my friend, you need to repent. This is hard to hear and hard to say, but the Bible says you're a murderer. You killed your own baby. You need to repent. Tell God you're sorry. His grace is more than enough to cover over this sin. But you need to acknowledge the sin. Confess your guilt and your shame, and ask God to forgive you. If Jesus has paid the price on the cross for your sins, he has paid the price for your abortion. Go to him.

I also want to encourage you to confess this sin to someone. Tell me. Tell another pastor. Tell a friend. Tell a sibling. Tell your parents. You may have been keeping this a secret for a long time. Telling someone will remove some of the burden you've been feeling. One day you may even be able to share your testimony, and God might just use that to accomplish something remarkable. He might use you to be a great force for good. He might use you to help babies be born who might otherwise be killed.

But friends, it's not just those of us who've had abortions who need to repent. All of us are guilty in some way. All of us should be doing more to prevent abortions. All of us, simply by buying in to the false Western ideals of individual autonomy, the so-called right to choose, and the right to privacy have contributed to creating a culture where abortion is rampant. All of us, by taking sex less seriously than we ought, by making sex outside of marriage acceptable and abstinence and purity prudish, old-fashioned, and lame have fostered a pro-choice society. Those of us who are married, who've consciously decided that we know best when we should become parents (for the first time or the second or third or fourth time) and leave God out of the equation have contributed to this problem. All of us need to repent. So, repent.

What else should we do? All of us should get educated and learn the facts. I've prepared a handout that you can take home.[6] Read one or two of the books that I've listed. Visit some of those web sites. Join one of those groups. Watch footage of an actual abortion. Your heart will break. You won't be able to stay silent any longer.

Get involved. Write to your Member of Parliament and encourage him or her to defend the defenseless. Start a pro-life group at your school. If you're married, adopt. There are so many unwanted children waiting for parents to love them. If you've been trying to get pregnant for a long time, before you consider fertility treatments, consider adopting. If God could adopt you into his family, you have every reason and motivation to adopt a child that he loves into yours.

Now, let me give you one thing you shouldn't do. Don't have sex. If you're married, ignore that. You can have as much sex as you want. With your spouse. Have babies. Have lots of babies. Love your children. But if you're not married, don't have sex until you are. If your boyfriend or girlfriend says they love you, tell them to wait. If they really love you, they will. If they won't—if they keep on pressuring you—kick them to the curb. Get a copy of this sermon and play this bit back to them. Kick. Them. To. The. Curb. Seriously. That guy isn't worth it. The book of Genesis tells us about a fellow named Jacob who served a man named

---

6. This handout includes a small sampling of some of the resources I discuss in Appendix B.

Laban for seven years so he could marry Laban's daughter, Rachel. And the Bible says that for Jacob, those seven years seemed like only a few days because of how much he loved her (Gen 29:20). Tell that guy to wait. Sex when you're married is awesome because you're not just giving your body to your spouse, you're giving everything to your spouse. You're completely open and vulnerable with each other. You aren't keeping anything from the other. Wait to have sex.

Now, if you choose to ignore me and you get pregnant—maybe you're pregnant right now—tell your parents. Don't be afraid of how they'll react. If they kick you out of their house, you can come and live with my family in Vancouver. I'm absolutely serious. Keep your baby. Or give her up for adoption. My wife and I will be happy to adopt your child, and there are others here who will, too, I know. Don't get an abortion. Please. I'm pleading with you on behalf of your baby. Don't get an abortion.

Conclusion

The Bible calls us to care for the weakest in the world; to rescue those who are being killed. Don't faint in the day of adversity. Don't look at the one hundred thousand babies being aborted in Canada every year and feel overwhelmed. Instead, find your hope and motivation in Christ. He didn't faint in the day of adversity. He went to the cross and he died. His death was the ultimate rescue for those who make him their treasure, who would otherwise be taken away to eternal death. Were it not for him, each of us would be lost. But he died so that we might be adopted into God's family. Do you know this Jesus? He knows you. He knows everything about you. He knows your deepest, darkest secrets. He knows the things you've said, the things you've done, the things you've thought. Does that terrify you? Don't let it. Because he not only knows you to the core, he loves you to the cross. The Bible says your sin, your complicity in abortion, drove Christ to the cross. He *had* to die for you. But the Bible also says that his love for you kept him on the cross. He died *for you*. He died to rescue you. Confess your sins to him. Ask him to save you. Then look to his love to give you the motivation and energy you need to go, and rescue the unborn.

Let's pray.

Father, thank you for Jesus. We are powerless to save ourselves, but you didn't leave us without hope. He came to rescue us, to save us from being eternally lost. Help us to find in the cross all the resources we need to go, with courage, into the world, telling people about the terrible sin of abortion and the amazing grace of your Son. May we not rest until abortion is seen in our country for what it is: an unspeakable crime against the unborn and against you. In Jesus' name we pray. Amen.

THE INCARNATION OF CHRIST

26In the sixth month the angel Gabriel was sent from God to a city of Galilee named Nazareth, 27to a virgin betrothed to a man whose name was Joseph, of the house of David. And the virgin's name was Mary. 28And he came to her and said, "Greetings, O favored one, the Lord is with you!" 29But she was greatly troubled at the saying, and tried to discern what sort of greeting this might be. 30And the angel said to her, "Do not be afraid, Mary, for you have found favor with God. 31And behold, you will conceive in your womb and bear a son, and you shall call his name Jesus. 32He will be great and will be called the Son of the Most High. And the Lord God will give to him the throne of his father David, 33and he will reign over the house of Jacob forever, and of his kingdom there will be no end."

34And Mary said to the angel, "How will this be, since I am a virgin?"

35And the angel answered her, "The Holy Spirit will come upon you, and the power of the Most High will overshadow you; therefore the child to be born will be called holy—the Son of God. 36And behold, your relative Elizabeth in her old age has also conceived a son, and this is the sixth month with her who was called barren. 37For nothing will be impossible with God." 38And Mary said, "Behold, I am the servant of the Lord; let it be to me according to your word." And the angel departed from her.

39In those days Mary arose and went with haste into the hill country, to a town in Judah, 40and she entered the house of Zechariah and greeted Elizabeth. 41And when Elizabeth heard the greeting of Mary, the baby leaped in her womb. And Elizabeth was filled with the Holy Spirit, 42and she exclaimed with a loud cry, "Blessed are you among women,

and blessed is the fruit of your womb! ⁴³*And why is this granted to me that the mother of my Lord should come to me?* ⁴⁴*For behold, when the sound of your greeting came to my ears, the baby in my womb leaped for joy.* ⁴⁵*And blessed is she who believed that there would be a fulfillment of what was spoken to her from the Lord."*
—Luke 1:26–45

March 25 is, maybe, the most important date on the Christian calendar.[7] That's strange, I can hear some of you thinking, surely I mean December 25. Christmas. The day Jesus was born. But, no, you heard me correctly. March 25. Why?

March 25 is the day the church has historically celebrated the Incarnation of Christ. The Incarnation is the Christian teaching that God, himself, became human. In North America we celebrate the Incarnation at Christmas, and for good reason. Christmas is the day that Jesus was born; the day he became visible to people on earth. But Jesus didn't simply drop into Mary's womb as a fully formed baby just waiting to be delivered.

Our passage this morning tells us that he was conceived by the Holy Spirit, as we recited together earlier in the Apostles' Creed, and developed, just as each of us here did, in his mother's womb until he was ready to be born nine months later. Before Jesus was a newborn, he was a fetus, an embryo, a zygote.

The question before us this morning is, So what? What difference does this make? What difference does the Incarnation make, practically, to how we live our lives?

And the answer, friends, is that the Incarnation makes all the difference in the world. The Incarnation changes everything.

Before we see how the Incarnation changes everything, and what this means for how we live, let me first address a question that many of you undoubtedly have. And that question is simply, is the Incarnation true? Did it really happen? How can Christians really believe that God

---

7. In this sermon (preached in my congregation on March 28, 2010) I purposely chose to keep specific appeals to apply the message at a minimum, opting instead to let listeners have more time to reflect theologically on the preached word. We talk about the sin of abortion frequently in my congregation so I decided to keep abortion-specific material at a greater distance here than in the previous sermon, above.

became a human being? Or to approach it from a different perspective: was Jesus really God in the flesh, or was he just another person? An exceptional, wise, compassionate person, maybe, but just another person.

This certainly isn't a question we can answer in the space of a few minutes. But there's no more important question to ask so we need to give it least some attention. If Jesus really is who he said he is, if he really is who the New Testament authors claim he is, that is, if he really is God incarnate, that should have a radical impact on how we live our lives. Jesus, himself, says that he came to forgive sins, to restore our broken relationship with God; or, to paraphrase *Jerry Maguire*, to complete us. To make us whole. To make us into the people we were made to be. The question of who Jesus is gets at the very heart of Christianity.

So, was Jesus really God in the flesh, or was he just a human being? There can be no doubt that there really was a human being named Jesus, who lived in a town called Nazareth, who did many of the things attributed to him in the Gospels. No one denies that he really existed. All historians, secular and Christian, agree that Jesus, the central figure of the Christian faith, really walked the earth. He's attested to in non-Christian writings from the first and early second centuries. Historians and scholars disagree on whether he was divine or simply human, but they all agree that he lived.

The question is, Who was he? Who is he?

Jesus claims that he has the power and authority to forgive sins (Mark 2:1–12); that he is eternally existent (John 8:58; 17:5); and that he will return to earth one day (John 14:3). What are we to do with these claims? The great Christian professor C. S. Lewis said there are only three possibilities. We can either call Jesus a lunatic, a liar, or the Lord. (Or as some have paraphrased, he was either mad, bad, or God.) What you can't do is call him a great moral teacher or simply the founder of another religion. Look closely at what Jesus claims. These aren't the claims of a great moral teacher. If what he says is true, then he is the Lord. He is God incarnate, God in the flesh. But if what he says is false, then he's a lunatic or a liar. What will you do with his claims?

There's more that can be said, of course. And many of you, I'm sure, have plenty of other questions. For now, though, may I ask you simply to have an open mind? To be open to the possibility that Jesus really is who he said he is? That if there is a God, that is, if God exists, that it would surely be possible for him to become a human being?

Our text, Luke 1:26–45, tells us this is what he did. He became a human being. Nine months before Christmas, an angel named Gabriel appeared to a young girl named Mary and told her that she would bear the Son of God.

Now there's something you should know about Mary. She would have been only twelve-years-old, maybe twelve-and-a-half, at this time.[8] Luke tells us she lived in a city called Nazareth. To be honest, "city" is a generous label. Nazareth was not so much a city as it was a small town. This is why Luke has to add that it's in Galilee. Galilee, his readers would have recognized, but they wouldn't have known Nazareth from Nanaimo.[9] So not only was Mary a pre-teen, she was a pre-teen from a small, middle-of-nowhere town.

She's going to be the mother of the Son of God?

Uh, are you sure, God? Wouldn't it make more sense to choose a woman from a well-to-do family? Someone with royal lineage, maybe? A successful business woman from the big city, perhaps, who's married to an influential man? In fact, why become a baby in a girl's womb to begin with? If you really need to become a human being, why not a grown adult? Why not a king? Or a warrior? Why a helpless fetus? And why this girl for a mother?

Can you imagine what a girl living today who's Mary's age and in Mary's situation would say if she found out she was pregnant?

1. My whole future is ahead of me. A baby would ruin my life.
2. It's only a few days old. I can still take emergency contraceptive pills and have it taken care of.
3. My figure will be ruined.
4. My parents will kill me.
5. I'll be embarrassed. Everyone at school will talk about me.
6. I can't afford to raise a baby.
7. I'm not ready to have a baby right now. I can't even take care of myself.

---

8. Bovon, *Luke*, 49.

9. Nanaimo is a small city on Vancouver Island, British Columbia, with a population under eighty thousand. Residents of the province will be familiar with it, but those outside of British Columbia, and certainly outside Canada, are unlikely to know it (though they may have tasted the eponymous chocolate dessert).

8. Joseph will dump me if I don't have an abortion.
9. I want kids one day, just not right now.
10. It's my body, it's my choice, and I don't want this baby.
11. It's not a girl, is it?
12. There are already too many people on this planet. We need to reduce our carbon footprint.

How does Mary respond?

Look at what she says: "I am the servant of the Lord; let it be to me according to your word" (v. 38). There's nothing at all about her so-called right to choose. Instead, she embraces the responsibility that God has given her. There's nothing at all about it being her body. Instead she says, in effect, "My body belongs to God" (1 Cor 6:19–20). There's nothing at all about how her life will be difficult, how her future will be compromised. Instead, she submits to God's plan for her life. She recognizes that God is in control of the situation.

She doesn't respond as we might expect someone like her to respond.

Now, Luke tells us in verse 27 that Mary was already betrothed to Joseph. Betrothal meant that she was already his wife in every way but sexually. She would have still been living with her parents, and in a year's time she would have gone to live in Joseph's home. Imagine what the reaction from Joseph and his community would have been when it was found that she was pregnant out of wedlock. Joseph knew he wasn't the father. Adultery in their day was severely punished. At best, Mary would have been on her own with no prospects for her future. No one would have married a known adulteress with a child. And women at that time had no real job prospects. Her future was grim and bleak.

But in the face of all this, Mary says, "I am the servant of the Lord; let it be to me according to you word." Remember, she's a pre-teen. What wisdom. What humility. What faith.

Would that more women today were like Mary. Would that more men were like her. Women and men who live not for themselves and their own pleasure and fulfillment, but for God.

After the angel leaves, Mary goes to see her cousin Elizabeth. Verse 39 tells us she "went with haste," which means she went straight away.[10]

---

10. See Johnson, *Gospel of Luke*, 40, and Marshall, *Gospel of Luke*, 79–80.

Elizabeth was, herself, an unusual mother. She was old, as was her husband, and yet she, too, conceived.

Now, when Mary came to see her, Elizabeth was six months pregnant with her child, John the Baptist. As soon as Mary greeted her at the door, Elizabeth's baby "leaped in her womb" (v. 41). Why? Elizabeth tells us. She says to Mary, "Blessed are you among women, and blessed is the fruit of your womb! And why is this granted to me that the mother of my Lord should come to me? For behold, when the sound of your greeting came to my ears, the baby in my womb leaped for joy" (vv. 42–44).

What can we observe from her words?

At least these five things.

First, God had to become human. He had to. Sin, the Bible says elsewhere, is so serious that it literally destroys the relationship with God that we were created to have. Sin is so serious that nothing less than the Son of God coming to earth to make atonement for our sin can repair and restore that broken relationship. Now that sounds harsh to some of you, I know. And we'll address the issue of sin in future weeks, so I hope you'll come back. But I just want you to see today, from this text, from the Incarnation of Christ, that God didn't come simply to show us he loves us. That's part of it, to be sure, but that's not all. He came to die.

The Incarnation is only the beginning of Jesus' earthly story. Good Friday is still to come. He had to die for our sins. But not only is Good Friday still to come, Easter is coming, too. Even death, the Bible says, can't separate those who love God from his love because on the very first Easter, Jesus destroyed death. He conquered it when he rose from the grave. He's still alive.

Second, notice that Mary is called blessed because of the child who's already living insider her: Jesus. None of us can be called blessed in the same way, but each of us can, nevertheless, be blessed, too, because Jesus is still alive, and if you confess your sin and your need for him to rescue you, he can, and will, live in you. He will make you new.

Third, Elizabeth is able to recognize Mary's baby as the Lord even though he's only a few days old. Luke tells us that Elizabeth lived in a town in Judah (v. 39), which was about a three or four day journey from Nazareth.[11] So Jesus is only three or four days old in the womb at this point. He's still a tiny, tiny embryo. And yet, he's already the Messiah. Don't skip over what Luke is teaching us here.

---

11. Green, *Gospel of Luke*, 94; Marshall, *Gospel of Luke*, 80.

This text has so much to tell us about the beginning of human life and, by consequence, our obligation to the youngest, frailest, most dependent among us. We don't become human beings at birth or at some arbitrary point during a woman's pregnancy, just as Jesus didn't become human at Christmas or during Mary's second or third trimester. We become human beings at conception, just as Jesus became a human being at his conception.

Fourth, look at the reaction of John the Baptist. He leaps in Elizabeth's womb at the mere sound of Mary's voice. This is so fascinating. Why would he leap? It must be because, despite being still three months away from being born, the Holy Spirit enabled him to perceive that Mary was pregnant with Jesus. He knew Jesus was there. The first meeting between John the Baptist and Jesus was a prenatal meeting. At the very least this tells us that there is much to prenatal life that is a mystery. There is much to how God operates in the life of an unborn child that we don't comprehend. But God is there from the very beginning, creating and caring for the growing, developing fetus.

Finally, notice not only that the prenatal John leaps, but that he leaps for joy (v. 44). This, ultimately, is the universal reaction of all who come to know and love the Lord Jesus. A joy that can't help but express itself.

If you don't know this Jesus, if you don't have this joy, I invite you this morning to consider Jesus in the womb. See him in his weakness and vulnerability. Only Christianity offers you a God who became abortable. You don't need to be afraid of this God. Take hold of him. Meet him. Don't wait until Christmas.

Let's pray.

Father, your Son came to earth not as a mighty man but as a microscopic zygote. He became weak to show us that we can only receive him in weakness, when we confess our inability to save ourselves. And thank you for Mary. She was most blessed. She experienced morning sickness, inexplicable cravings for strange foods, sang songs to the baby in her womb, dreamed dreams for what he might become. For nine months she carried our Lord in her belly. For nine months she was his home. For nine months she nurtured and protected the one who came to rescue even her. Might more of us come to know and love the child she birthed, the child she loved, the child who came to save sinners. In his name we pray. Amen.

Epilogue

> *"This," cried the Mayor, "is your town's darkest hour!*
> *The time for all Whos who have blood that is red*
> *To come to the aid of their country!" he said.*
> *"We've GOT to make noises in greater amounts!*
> *So, open your mouth, lad! For every voice counts!"*
>
> —Dr. Seuss

When Horton tries to tell the other animals in the jungle that life exists on the tiny speck he's safeguarding, that it's really a little world called Who-ville, not only is he mocked and derided, but the other animals become angry and plot to stop him. They capture him and take the speck, not believing that it's inhabited by microscopic life.

Horton has no ally except the Mayor of Who-ville. Like Horton, however, the Mayor's attempts to convince his people that danger is imminent are met with laughter and unbelief. But he persists. He pleads. He persuades. In the end they cry out with all their voices, and it works. The animals hear the shouting of the Whos, and they are rescued.

Like the Whos, the unborn need someone to intervene. They're so small (and still forming) that many have a hard time thinking of them as people. The Whos had an advocate pleading their case, but ultimately, it was their voices that saved the day. The unborn, however, are voiceless. They sense danger but they can't cry out. They feel pain but they can't scream. They need us to persist, to plead, to persuade, to pray.

And they need us to preach. O! how they need us to preach.

I pray you will take up this challenge.

Appendix A

Nursing and Feeding: Equipping the Church for Pro-Life Ministry

Most people who say they oppose abortion do just enough to salve the conscience but not enough to stop the killing.

—Gregg Cunningham

My goal in this short appendix is to suggest some ideas worth implementing in your congregation. Some of these ideas are proactive strategies, some are reactive. Some may not be doable in your church. Others can be implemented tomorrow. I hope you will consider them and take them further than what I've sketched so briefly here. For the most part these are simply initial thoughts. I don't presume to know everything there is to know about mobilizing the church for pro-life work. In my own congregation we're just beginning this discussion. Still, here are ten places we can start.

1. Preach it! Preach on abortion often. As long as abortion is a legal and common procedure, you can't preach on it enough. If your people aren't complaining that you speak too often about abortion, you're probably not addressing it as often as you should. When they do tell you they think you're talking about abortion too frequently, gently explain to them why it's necessary. Few things will encourage your people to work against abortion like having their pastor tell them about the importance of doing so.

2. During your worship service, have someone share a pro-life testimony. Invite someone from a crisis pregnancy center to tell about the work they're doing and offer ways for your people to be in-

volved. Or have a post-abortive woman or man share their story with the congregation and tell people about the personal devastation abortion causes.

3. Organize a group of parishioners to picket outside an abortion clinic. Establish meaningful partnerships with some other churches in your city and make this an inter-congregation event. Don't just be a part of this team, direct it. Your people want to see you living out what you preach. Lead them with both your words and your actions. While we're on the subject, partnering with other churches and pro-life groups will be an important strategy in changing the abortion culture in your city. Would that more churches hear this message.[1]

4. Encourage political action. Urge your people to write letters. Simplify the process for them by creating a standard form letter that they can simply fill out with their personal information. Give your people a list of public officials' phone numbers and tell them to call and make their voices heard. When a "March for Life" is in your area, have your church take part.

5. Start a group for parents thinking about adoption. Put your money where your mouth is by designating funds in the budget to helping families with the costly adoption process.[2]

6. Start a group for those interested in learning more about abortion and other ethical issues like euthanasia. Invite pro-choice adherents and doctors, in particular. The more of these folks you can persuade to become pro-life, the further the cause will be advanced. If you're a student, start a pro-life group at school.

7. Designate a group of deacons to be specifically responsible for post-abortive counseling within your local church. Invite a professional counselor to come and train your people, and tell your congregation about the availability of this service. While you're at it, budget funds for people who need post-abortive counseling but can't afford to pay for it.

---

1. See the ministry of Churches for Life (www.getintolife.org), for a helpful model of one way to do this.

2. See, for example, the wonderful, life-affirming ministry of Heartbeat International.

8. Start a home for women in crisis pregnancies if one doesn't already exist in your community. This is a capital-intensive project and no small undertaking. But in my experience, there is, sadly, always a need for more such safe homes. Consider joining with other churches and pro-life groups in your community and coming up with some fundraising ideas and events.

9. Resources! When you preach on abortion, prepare a handout listing the local pro-life groups where your congregation can get involved. Make sure your church library is adequately stocked with quality pro-life pamphlets, books, and videos.

10. Set aside a day to fast and pray for pro-life ministries. Spotlight these ministries during announcement times. This may be a good way to get kids involved. Explain to them what you're doing and why you're doing it.[3]

These are a handful of ways you can mobilize your church for pro-life work. I pray that your church will find some of them worth trying, that you will come up with new ideas of your own, and that together we will take up the pro-life banner and work to end abortion, for the glory of God.

---

3. Frank Pavone offers some suggestions on addressing abortion from the pulpit with children in "Preaching to Children About Abortion," 57–60.

Appendix B

For Further Reading: A Bibliographic Essay

> To take a stand . . . about abortion as a moral issue is also to take a stand against the principal currents and trends which we have inherited from nineteenth-century industry. . . . It is the decline of the human significance resulting from industrial goals and methods that now confronts both the exponents and the victims of abortion. Caught between the industrial quantitative values and the new life values of the electric age, many people are unable to perceive why they feel so unhappy about abortions while at the same time thinking that it is a plausible and enlightened program for the relief of man's congested estate.
>
> —Marshall McLuhan

The purpose of this brief essay is to highlight resources for those interested in learning more about abortion. This isn't a comprehensive collection by any means, but a representative survey of some of the best material available.

OVERVIEW

A great place to begin is with an overview of abortion. Terry Schlossberg and Elizabeth Achtemeier's *Not My Own: Abortion and the Marks of the Church* (Grand Rapids: Eerdmans, 1995) examines preaching, baptism, the Lord's Supper, church discipline, and ministries of service, and what role each plays with respect to abortion. A more general introduction to abortion is found in R. C. Sproul's *Abortion: A Rational Look at An Emotional Issue*, 2nd ed. (Orlando: Reformation Trust, 2010). John Jefferson Davis's *Abortion and the Christian: What Every Believer Should*

Know (Phillipsburg, NJ: Presbyterian and Reformed, 1984), though dated, remains a valuable starting point. Davis is a theology professor at Gordon-Conwell Theological Seminary who has lectured extensively on biblical ethics. His *Evangelical Ethics: Issues Facing the Church Today*, 3rd ed. (Phillipsburg, NJ: P & R, 2004) is a helpful book that addresses abortion, as well as a number of other issues, including contraception, divorce and remarriage, homosexuality, euthanasia, and capital punishment.

Richard Hays approaches ethics from the perspective of a New Testament scholar in *The Moral Vision of the New Testament: Community, Cross, New Creation; A Contemporary Introduction to New Testament Ethics* (New York: HarperSanFrancisco, 1996). The book is divided into four parts, each focusing on a different task in the study of New Testament ethics. Hays demonstrates how to read the ethical writings of the New Testament; the legitimacy of finding "a unity of ethical perspectives within the diversity of the canon" (4); how to move hermeneutically from the world of the Bible to our own context; and what the New Testament ethical world has to tell us about contemporary ethical issues such as abortion. It will reward careful reading.

One of the most comprehensive treatments of Christian ethics is John Frame's *The Doctrine of the Christian Life* (Phillipsburg, NJ: P & R, 2008), the third volume in his "A Theology of Lordship" series. This is a massive tome at over one thousand pages, but full of wisdom and scholarship, written in an accessible manner. Frame also addresses beginning- and end-of-life issues in *Medical Ethics: Principles, Persons, and Problems* (Phillipsburg, NJ: Presbyterian & Reformed, 1988). His *Perspectives on the Word of God: An Introduction to Christian Ethics* (Phillipsburg, NJ: Presbyterian and Reformed, 1990), a series of lectures he gave at Trinity Evangelical Divinity School in 1988, is a helpful initiation into his multi-perspectival approach to knowledge.

Bernard Nathanson writes about abortion from a unique vantage point. Nathanson was a former abortion doctor, founder of the pro-choice *National Association for the Repeal of Abortion Laws*, and the former director of the largest abortion clinic in the world. He presided over tens of thousands of abortions during his career, before changing his mind, in large part due to ultrasound imaging technology. *Aborting America* (Garden City, NY: Doubleday, 1979), which he co-authored with Richard Ostling, recounts his first-hand experience as an abortionist, and how he became a pro-life advocate. In *The Hand of God: A Journey from Death to*

Life by the Abortion Doctor Who Changed His Mind (Washington, DC: Regnery, 1996) Nathanson goes into further detail.

The best source on the history of abortion in the United States is Marvin Olasky's *Abortion Rites: A Social History of Abortion in America* (Wheaton, IL: Crossway, 1992). Michael Gorman studies abortion with a different historical interest in his *Abortion and the Early Church: Christian, Jewish and Pagan Attitudes in the Greco-Roman World* (Downers Grove, IL: InterVarsity, 1982). Gorman examines the earliest Christian attitudes toward abortion and argues, convincingly, that the early church was in universal agreement in condemning abortion. His exhaustive treatment of primary sources makes this a very valuable tool.

Another historical work worth consulting is *Prolife Feminism: Yesterday and Today* (New York: Sulzburger & Graham, 1995), edited by Rachel MacNair, Mary Krane Derr, and Linda Naranjo-Huebl. Primary writings from well-known feminists such as Charlotte Denman Lozier, Elizabeth Cady Stanton, Susan B. Anthony, and many others demonstrate that historically, those who've borne the title of "feminist" have been pro-life. This anthology helpfully shows that a person need not be a misogynist to be anti-abortion; that, in fact, it is "pro-woman" to be pro-life. In a similar vein, pastors may also wish to consult *The Cost of "Choice": Women Evaluate the Impact of Abortion* (San Francisco: Encounter, 2004), edited by Erika Bachiochi, featuring a dozen essays from female doctors, lawyers, ethicists, and professors.

A WOMAN'S PERSPECTIVE

Indeed, reading the perspective of women on abortion can be extremely helpful for both men and women who've not had any direct involvement with it. Consider, for instance, Noreen Riols's description of her post-abortion grief in *My Unknown Child: A Personal Story of Abortion* ([London: Hodder & Stoughton, 1995], 4):

> In an abortion there are always two victims: the baby who dies, but also the mother, who has to live the rest of her life with her guilt and remorse. When my baby died something died in me also and I am sure I am not alone in this. The terrible thing is that it is irrevocable. All the tears in the world won't bring the baby back. Jesus can heal and forgive us, and he will if we ask him. But the consequences of an abortion remain. We have to live with the memory of our unknown child, the baby who might have been.

Preachers who tell women they should no longer feel bad about their abortions after having confessed and received Christ's forgiveness need to read Riols. Being forgiven doesn't erase the consequences of sin, especially this sin.

Or consider Phyllis Tickle's painfully personal insight into a woman's grief over miscarriage, in her essay "What We Would Like You to Know" (10–11):

> I could never so reduce the memories of the swirling waters carrying my children away to sewage plants, nor could the shadows of their presence ever be exorcised from the dining tables of Christmases and Thanksgivings, of birthdays and anniversaries. They still remain, like Banquo's ghost, as tangible and informative as any idea appertained, and as realized. It is they who persuade me that only women can bring to the issue of abortion not only the tools with which to conduct the debate, but the anguish out of which to sanctify it.

It is hard, if not impossible, for a man to fully identify with the intensity of emotion a woman who's had an abortion (or lost a child through miscarriage) experiences. Reading women in their own voice helps to bridge this gender gap somewhat. Tickle's words, for instance, allow the reader to understand something of the painful, lingering memories that continue to haunt many women who've lost children through unintentional miscarriage or deliberate abortion. We shouldn't assume these feelings go away, or even diminish, with time.

Tickle's essay is the preface to a collection of essays she edited titled *Confessing Conscience: Churched Women on Abortion* (Nashville: Abingdon, 1990). Twelve different women from different vocations contribute to this volume. Not all are opposed to abortion, though all are professing Christians. The essays are of varying quality, as one would expect from a project with so many collaborators.

Frederica Mathews-Green also concentrates on women in *Real Choices: Listening to Women; Looking for Alternatives to Abortion* (Ben Lomond, CA: Conciliar, 1997). She seeks to identify the different reasons women choose to have abortions, and then suggests things that need to be done to change that reality. Among her answers: preventing unplanned pregnancies; men learning to be fathers; parents learning to be parents; welfare reform and improved employment plans allowing mothers increased flexibility to work *and* parent; and adoption. Her stated goal is to help the two sides in the abortion debate to work together (177–78):

> For more than two-decades, pro-lifers have presumed that the great silent middle was our best ally in the fight against abortion. But the middle appears to have been cornered by the two sides' rhetoric into simultaneously agreeing that abortion is child-murder and wishing it to remain legal, a position so exhausting in its illogic that they prefer not to think about it at all. The bored and reluctant middle is not the pro-life movement's best ally. Instead, pro-choicers are.

It is a provocative thesis. She observes that some pro-choice proponents have much in common with many in the pro-life camp. If we really want to end abortion "we must first demonstrate that it is possible to live without abortion, that we can find ways to prevent unwanted pregnancies or, failing that, to support them" (178). This, Mathewes-Green argues, will take working together.

Not every pro-choice advocate, however, agrees with Mathewes-Green that the number of abortions in America should be reduced. *Abortion: My Choice, God's Grace; Christian Women Tell Their Stories* (Pasadena: New Paradigm, 1994), edited by Anne Eggebroten, is a collection of essays by women who profess to be both Christians and pro-choice. These women want to keep abortion legal. Of particular note is a chapter by Claudia Davis titled "A Pastor's Wife Faces Truth" (73–84), in which she describes how her husband suggested she abort their first child (which she did) when she became pregnant while he was a seminary student. She recounts, too, that her counselor at the Planned Parenthood abortion clinic was a member of the United Methodist Church. These essays will rouse feelings of anger and sadness, and stir you up to preach against abortion.

APOLOGETICS

Where do we begin addressing the pro-choice views espoused by people like the contributors to Eggebroten's and Davis's volumes? Preachers do well to start with Scott Klusendorf's *The Case for Life: Equipping Christians to Engage the Culture* (Wheaton, IL: Crossway, 2009). Klusendorf articulates a remarkably simple but logical and effective plan for dialoguing with abortion choice proponents. He covers virtually every argument you're likely to encounter. Klusendorf has also designed a five-part DVD small group study with Gregory Koukl called *Making Abortion Unthinkable: The Art of Pro-Life Persuasion*, which is a terrific interactive training program. Francis Beckwith's *Politically Correct Death: Answering Arguments for Abortion Rights* (Grand Rapids: Baker, 1993) is another valuable apologetic resource. Beckwith is a first-class philosopher, and his apologetic skill is on full display in this book, as well as his more recent *Defending Life: A Moral and Legal Case Against Abortion Choice* (New York: Cambridge University Press, 2007), where he ably argues for the fetus as "a full-fledged member of the human community" (xii). Randy Alcorn's *Prolife Answers to Prochoice Arguments*, rev. ed. (Sisters, OR: Multnomah, 2000) covers much of the same ground as Klusendorf and Beckwith, but is also worth consulting, as is Jean Staker Garton's *Who Broke the Baby?: What the Abortion Slogans Really Mean* (Minneapolis: Bethany House, 1979).

James Tunstead Burtchaell, a former president of the American Academy of Religion and professor at the University of Notre Dame, addresses abortion from a Catholic perspective in *Rachel Weeping: The Case Against Abortion* (New York: Harper & Row, 1984). The book contains five essays on abortion, including two that compare abortion to the Holocaust and to slavery. It is an excellent scholarly work.

The slavery-abortion analogy is made well by J. C. Willke in *Abortion and Slavery: History Repeats* (Cincinnati: Hayes, 1984). Both slaves and fetuses are treated as non-persons and as the property of another who's free to choose whether to buy or sell (in slavery) or keep or kill (in abortion).

Michael Gorman and Ann Loar Brooks's *Holy Abortion?: A Theological Critique of the Religious Coalition for Reproductive Choice; Why Christians and Christian Churches Should Reconsider the Issue of Abortion* (Eugene, OR: Wipf and Stock, 2003) is an apologetic against the views of the Religious Coalition for Reproductive Choice, a group that, in Gorman and Brooks's words, "treats abortion as a holy, moral, liberating, empowering, divine gift and right" (33).

COUNSELING

Once you begin to preach on abortion you may soon find yourself counseling women who've had abortions and men who've encouraged them. Two helpful counseling resources are Terry Selby and Marc Bockmon's *The Mourning After: Help for the Postabortion Syndrome* (Grand Rapids: Baker, 1990), and Guy Condon and David Hazard's *Fatherhood Aborted:*

The Profound Effects of Abortion on Men (Wheaton, IL: Tyndale House, 2001). Both books have been helpful to me in my own ministry.

Selby and Bockmon focus on women suffering from post-abortion syndrome. They help pastor-counselors deal with a woman's denial, grief, and sense of victimization. Condon and Hazard's book is one of the few dealing primarily with men and abortion. You may be surprised at how many men feel a profound sense of shame and guilt over their culpability in the killing of their unborn children. This book will help you counsel them. Also useful is Michael Mannion's *Abortion and Healing: A Cry to be Whole* (Kansas City, MO: Sheed & Ward, 1986), written from a Catholic perspective.

Finally, I need to mention the work of David Powlison and the folks at the Christian Counseling and Educational Foundation (CCEF). Their work, particularly their insights into the human heart and their application of the gospel to our problems, is eminently relevant to abortion-related counseling. Start with Powlison's *Seeing with New Eyes: Counseling and the Human Condition Through the Lens of Scripture* (Phillipsburg, NJ: P & R, 2003), part of CCEF's "Resources for Changing Lives" series. But also be sure to make copies of their booklet *Healing After Abortion: God's Mercy Is for You* (Greensboro, NC: New Growth, 2008) available to those in your church who need it.

TAKING ACTION

In addition to counseling, several books (though not nearly enough) suggest ways to be involved in pro-life work at various levels. Let me commend a few to you. *52 Simple Things You Can Do To Be Pro-Life*, by Anne Pierson and Carol Risser, is a short primer that's packed with practical ideas. In addition to the fifty-two simple things from the book's title, the authors also offer seven additional ideas for those interested in being more involved. *Arresting Abortion: Practical Ways to Save Unborn Children*, Rutherford Institute Report 4 (Westchester, IL: Crossway, 1985), edited by John Whitehead, consists of eight essays by different contributors, offering a variety of ideas for combating abortion. Chapter 5, "LIGHT House" by Marilyn Lewis (66–82), describes the ministry of a home specifically designed to help women with unplanned pregnancies. If more churches and Christian leaders captured the vision laid out here, I believe there would be fewer abortions performed each year.

Randall Hekman also offers some ideas on how to end abortion in *Justice for the Unborn: Why We Have "Legal" Abortion and How We Can Stop It* (Ann Arbor, MI: Servant, 1984). Hekman is a judge, and describes his decision to deny a thirteen-year-old girl's petition to have a court-ordered abortion. He writes in his ruling, "There is no question in my mind that if I am ordered to initiate procedures to kill innocent life for the expediency of otheres [sic], that that is a 'criminal order' which I cannot obey" (164–65). Although Hekman focuses primarily on legal approaches to end abortion, this is a very readable book with useful ideas for anyone interested.

Mark Belz makes the case for civil disobedience in *Suffer the Little Children: Christians, Abortion, and Civil Disobedience* (Westchester, IL: Crossway, 1989). He cites examples from the Bible of people who opposed unjust governments (think for instance of Daniel, Shadrach, Meshach, and Abednego) and argues that Christians aren't just permitted by Scripture to participate in non-violent acts of civil disobedience, but have a duty to do so when it comes to abortion. We should protest at the doors of abortion clinics. To bolster his argument, he describes his reaction to watching an actual abortion in the film *Assignment Life* (74–75):

> When I saw the abortionist getting ready to insert the needle into the mother's abdomen, my reaction (even though I knew I was watching a movie) was immediate and real. I found myself wanting to be there, to pull the syringe out of the doctor's hand, to restrain the man from this murder, to protect the helpless, unsuspecting child. I was not thinking about legal issues or about constitutional rights. I found myself just reacting in a visceral sort of way to the awful injustice that was taking place before my eyes. It was obvious to me that that man had no right to do what he was doing. The baby was innocent and cornered, without a chance. He was locked in his mother's womb, a death sentence upon him, with no one but barbarians (or very confused people) in the room. The baby had no one to stand up for his life, no one to intervene.
>
> That is why a man is brought to the point that he blocks a door. It is because of the baby. He attempts to forbid entrance of a pregnant woman to an abortion clinic, even to the extent of violating the law, in order to save the child's life . . . to do what he can to protect and preserve the life of the unborn child who is only moments away from death.

Randy Alcorn also examines civil disobedience in *Is Rescuing Right? Breaking the Law to Save the Unborn* (Downers Grove, IL: InterVarsity, 1990). His conclusion (235):

> Not all of us in the church will be called upon by our Lord to do the same thing in the same way. All of us can, however, be supportive of sacrificial intervention that gives credibility to our words. This must involve much more than peaceful civil disobedience at abortion clinics to save the lives of unborn children. But surely it can include it.

These are wise and compelling words.

WEB SITES

In addition to these printed resources, the Internet is a trove of pro-life treasures, though you'll need to wade through some less valuable material to find them. Here to help you on your way are six trustworthy sites.

1. Abort73.com, an outstanding abortion education web site aimed at young people. Their mission statement reads:

   > Motivated by our Christian calling to establish justice, to expose evil injustices, to minister to the needy and helpless, and to extend love to every human person, Abort73.com aims to expose the practice of abortion as an injustice of historic proportions. We believe the best way to do so is to persistently, creatively, and comprehensively educate individuals (esp. students) with the massive body of evidence that stands against it. We strategically target a young audience (e.g., high school and college students) and are taking full advantage of the technology available to educate as many people as possible (i.e., the internet). We think it is good and necessary to use both secular and theological arguments to make our case against the practice of abortion. Since abortion claims the lives of thousands of the helpless unborn everyday and millions every year, we cannot do nothing.

2. AbortionNo.org, the web site for the Center for Bio-Ethical Reform, an organization that uses graphic abortion images to convince people that a real human being is killed every time an abortion is performed.

3. AfterAbortion.org, an online resource specializing in post-abortion issues. They also serve as the web host for the online journal *The Post-Abortion Review*.

4. CBHD.org, the web site of the Center for Bioethics and Human Diversity, the bioethics research center of Trinity International University in Deerfield, IL.

5. LifeSiteNews.com, a news portal whose "purpose is to provide balance and more accurate coverage on culture, life and family matters than is usually given by other media."

6. ProLifeTraining.com, the web site of the Life Training Institute (LTI), founded by Scott Klusendorf. LTI's mission is to train "pro-life advocates to persuasively defend their views in the marketplace of ideas."

Finally, visit ProLifePulpit.com, the online home of this book, for additional resources, including links to other helpful web sites, abortion-related news, study guides, and more.

CONCLUSION

I encourage you to continue learning about abortion. Start with some of the sources here in one or more of the areas that interests you. Then continue reading as you discover new resources and unearth fresh material. Your pro-life pastoral ministry will be stronger because of it.

Bibliography

Achtemeier, Elizabeth. "Speaking the Unspeakable: A Demonstration." In *The Right Choice: Pro-Life Sermons from . . .*, edited by Paul T. Stallswoth, 19–27. Nashville: Abingdon, 1997.
Adam, Mary B. "Strategies for Sex Education." In *BioEngagement: Making a Christian Difference through Bioethics Today*, edited by Nigel M. de S. Cameron et al., 80–88. Grand Rapids: Eerdmans, 2000.
Adams, Jay E. *Handbook of Church Discipline*. Grand Rapids: Zondervan, 1974.
———. *Preaching With Purpose: The Urgent Task of Homiletics*. Phillipsburg, NJ: Presbyterian and Reformed, 1982.
Alcorn, Randy. *Prolife Answers to Prochoice Arguments*. Rev. ed. Sisters, OR: Multnomah, 2000.
Alcorn, Randy C. *Is Rescuing Right?: Breaking the Law to Save the Unborn*. Downers Grove, IL: InterVarsity, 1990.
Bachiochi, Erika, ed. *The Cost of "Choice": Women Evaluate the Impact of Abortion*. San Francisco: Encounter, 2004.
Barth, Karl. *Church Dogmatics*. Translated by G. W. Bromiley, et al. Edited by G. W. Bromiley and T. F. Torrance. Vol. 3, bk. 20. London: T & T Clark, 2009.
Bash, Anthony. *Ambassadors for Christ: An Exploration of Ambassadorial Language in the New Testament*. Wissenschaftliche Untersuchungen zum Neuen Testament 2/92. Tübingen: Mohr (Siebeck), 1997.
Basil. *Letters*. Translated by Agnes Clarke Way. Fathers of the Church 2. Washington, DC: Catholic University of America Press, 1955.
Baxter, Richard. "Cases and Directions for Loving Our Neighbour As Ourselves." In *The Practical Works of Richard Baxter*, vol. 1, 870–73. Morgan, PA: Soli Deo Gloria, 2000.
———. *The Reformed Pastor*. Edited by William Brown. Edinburgh: Banner of Truth Trust, 1989.
Becker, Ernest. *The Denial of Death*. New York: Simon & Schuster, 1973.
Beckwith, Francis J. *Defending Life: A Moral and Legal Case Against Abortion Choice*. New York: Cambridge University Press, 2007.
———. *Politically Correct Death: Answering Arguments for Abortion Rights*. Grand Rapids: Baker, 1993.
Belz, Mark. *Suffer the Little Children: Christians, Abortion, and Civil Disobedience*. Westchester, IL: Crossway, 1989.
Blackburn, Susan Tucker. *Maternal, Fetal, and Neonatal Physiology: A Clinical Perspective*. 3rd ed. St. Louis: Saunders, 2007.
Bock, Darrell. *Luke: Volume 2; 9:51–24:53*. Baker Exegetical Commentary on the New Testament. Grand Rapids: Baker, 1994.

Bonhoeffer, Dietrich. *Ethics*. Translated by Reinhard Krauss, et al. Edited by Clifford J. Green. Dietrich Bonhoeffer Works 6. Minneapolis: Fortress, 2005.

Bovon, François. *Luke 1: A Commentary on the Gospel of Luke 1:1–9:50*. Translated by Christine M. Thomas. Edited by Helmut Koester. Hermeneia. Minneapolis: Fortress, 2002.

Boyd, Brian. "The Origin of Stories: *Horton Hears a Who.*" *Philosophy and Literature* 25 (2001): 197–214.

Brown, Detine Lee. "A Strange Speech of an Estranged People: Theory and Practice of Antebellum African-American Freedom Day Orations." PhD diss., Purdue University, 1992.

Brueggemann, Walter. "Psalms and the Life of Faith: A Suggested Typology of Function." *Journal for the Study of the Old Testament* 17 (1980): 3–32.

Bunge, Marcia J., et al., eds. *The Child in the Bible*. Grand Rapids: Eerdmans, 2008.

Bunyan, John. *The Pilgrim's Progress*. Oxford: Oxford University Press, 1945.

Burtchaell, James Tunstead. *Rachel Weeping: The Case Against Abortion*. New York: Harper & Row, 1984.

Caird, G. B. *Saint Luke*. Westminster Pelican Commentaries. Philadelphia: Westminster, 1977.

Calvin, John. *Commentaries on the Last Four Books of Moses, Arranged in the Form of A Harmony*. Translated by Charles William Bingham. Vol. 3. Grand Rapids: Baker, 1950.

Canadian Centre for Bio-Ethical Reform. "Frequently Asked Questions about the Reproductive 'Choice' Campaign." No pages. Online: http://www.unmaskingchoice.ca/rcc-FAQ.html.

Cargal, Timothy B. *Hearing a Film, Seeing a Sermon: Preaching and Popular Movies*. Louisville: Westminster John Knox, 2007.

Chang, Curtis. *Engaging Unbelief: A Captivating Strategy from Augustine and Aquinas*. Downers Grove, IL: InterVarsity, 2000.

Chapell, Bryan. *Christ-Centered Preaching: Redeeming the Expository Sermon*. 2nd ed. Grand Rapids: Baker Academic, 2005.

Childers, Jana. Introduction to *Birthing the Sermon: Women Preachers on the Creative Process*, edited by Jana Childers, ix–x. St. Louis: Chalice, 2001.

Childs, James M., Jr. *Preaching Justice: The Ethical Vocation of Word and Sacrament Ministry*. Harrisburg, PA: Trinity, 2000.

Chrysostom, John. "Homily 24 on Romans." No pages. Online: http://www.newadvent.org/fathers/210224.htm.

Clowney, Edmund P. *Called to the Ministry*. Phillipsburg, NJ: Presbyterian and Reformed, 1964.

———. *Preaching Christ in All of Scripture*. Wheaton, IL: Crossway, 2003.

Cobb, John B., Jr. *Progressive Christians Speak: A Different Voice on Faith and Politics*. Louisville: Westminster John Knox, 2002.

Condon, Guy, and David Hazard. *Fatherhood Aborted: The Profound Effects of Abortion on Men*. Carol Stream, IL: Tyndale House, 2001.

Craddock, Fred B. *Luke*. Interpretation. Louisville: John Knox, 1990.

Craven, Erma Clardy. "Abortion, Poverty and Black Genocide: Gifts to the Poor?" In *Abortion and Social Justice*, edited by Thomas W. Hilgers and Dennis J. Horan, 231–43. New York: Sheed & Ward, 1972.

Crisp, Oliver D. *God Incarnate: Explorations in Christology*. London: T & T Clark, 2009.

Davidson, Robert. *The Vitality of Worship: A Commentary on the Book of Psalms*. Grand Rapids: Eerdmans; Edinburgh: Handsel, 1998.
Davis, Ellen F. *Proverbs, Ecclesiastes, and the Song of Songs*. Westminster Bible Companion. Louisville: Westminster John Knox, 2000.
Davis, John Jefferson. *Abortion and the Christian: What Every Believer Should Know*. Phillipsburg, NJ: Presbyterian and Reformed, 1984.
―――. *Evangelical Ethics: Issues Facing the Church Today*. 3rd ed. Phillipsburg, NJ: P & R, 2004.
Department of Justice Canada. "Criminal Code of Canada, Part VIII: Offences Against the Person and Reputation." No pages. Online: http://laws-lois.justice.gc.ca/eng/acts/C-46/page-148.html.
Dever, Mark. *Nine Marks of a Healthy Church*. 2nd ed. Wheaton, IL: Crossway, 2004.
Dever, Mark, and Paul Alexander. *The Deliberate Church: Building Your Ministry on the Gospel*. Wheaton, IL: Crossway, 2005.
Dewan, Shaila. "To Court Blacks, Foes of Abortion Make Racial Case." No pages. Online: http://www.nytimes.com/2010/02/27/us/27race.html.
Di Mauro, Dennis. *A Love for Life: Christianity's Consistent Protection of the Unborn*. Eugene, OR: Wipf & Stock, 2008.
Doehring, Carrie. "Using Literature as Case Studies." In *Taking Care: Monitoring Power Dynamics and Relational Boundaries in Pastoral Care and Counseling*, 141–52. Nashville: Abingdon, 1995.
Drash, Wayne. "The abortionist and his No. 1 foe." No pages. Online: http://www.cnn.com/2009/US/10/27/abortion.war/index.html.
Edwards, Jonathan. "Gospel Ministers A Savor of Life or Of Death." In *The Works of Jonathan Edwards, vol. 22: Sermons and Discourses, 1739–1742*, edited by Harry S. Stout, 205–10. New Haven: Yale University Press, 2003.
―――. "The True Excellency of A Minister of the Gospel." In *The Works of Jonathan Edwards, vol. 25: Sermons and Discourses, 1743–1758*, edited by Wilson H. Kimnach, 84–102. New Haven: Yale University Press, 2006.
Eggebroten, Anne, ed. *Abortion: My Choice, God's Grace; Christian Women Tell Their Stories*. Pasadena: New Paradigm, 1994.
Elshtain, Jean Bethke. "A Cultural Disorder: C. S. Lewis and the Abolition of Man." In *A Report from the Front Lines: Conversations on Public Theology; A Festschrift in Honor of Robert Benne*, edited by Michael Shahan, 35–46. Grand Rapids: Eerdmans, 2009.
Enouen, Susan W. "Planned Parenthood Abortion Facilities Target African American Communities." No pages. Online: http://www.lifeissues.org/connector/display.asp?page=05oct.htm.
ESV Study Bible. Wheaton, IL: Crossway, 2008.
Fitzmyer, Joseph A. *The Gospel according to Luke X–XXIV*. Anchor Bible 28A. Garden City, NY: Doubleday, 1985.
Forbes, Bruce David. "Introduction: Finding Religion in Unexpected Places." In *Religion and Popular Culture in America*. Rev. ed., edited by Bruce David Forbes and Jeffrey H. Mahan, 1–20. Berkeley: University of California Press, 2005.
Frame, John M. *The Doctrine of the Christian Life*. A Theology of Lordship. Phillipsburg, NJ: P & R, 2008.
―――. *Medical Ethics: Principles, Persons, and Problems*. Phillipsburg, NJ: Presbyterian and Reformed, 1988.

———. *Perspectives on the Word of God: An Introduction to Christian Ethics*. Phillipsburg, NJ: Presbyterian and Reformed, 1990.

Garton, Jean Staker. *Who Broke the Baby?: What the Abortion Slogans Really Mean.* Minneapolis: Bethany House, 1979.

Gilstrap, Michael R. *The Phineas Report*. Tyler, TX: Geneva Divinity School Press, 1983.

Godawa, Brian. *Hollywood Worldviews: Watching Films with Wisdom and Discernment*. Downers Grove, IL: InterVarsity, 2002.

Goldsworthy, Graeme. *Preaching the Whole Bible as Christian Scripture: The Application of Biblical Theology to Expository Preaching*. Grand Rapids: Eerdmans, 2000.

Gordon, T. David. *Why Johnny Can't Preach: The Media Have Shaped the Messengers*. Phillipsburg, NJ: P & R, 2009.

Gorman, Michael J. *Abortion and the Early Church: Christian, Jewish and Pagan Attitudes in the Greco-Roman World*. Downers Grove, IL: InterVarsity, 1982.

Gorman, Michael J., and Ann Loar Brooks. *Holy Abortion?: A Theological Critique of the Religious Coalition for Reproductive Choice; Why Christians and Christian Churches Should Reconsider the Issue of Abortion*. Eugene, OR: Wipf & Stock, 2003.

Green, Joel B. *The Gospel of Luke*. New International Commentary on the New Testament. Grand Rapids: Eerdmans, 1997.

Greidanus, Sidney. *The Modern Preacher and the Ancient Text: Interpreting and Preaching Biblical Literature*. Grand Rapids: Eerdmans, 1988.

———. *Preaching Christ from the Old Testament: A Contemporary Hermeneutical Model*. Grand Rapids: Eerdmans, 1999.

Hauerwas, Stanley. "Abortion, Theologically Understood." In *The Hauerwas Reader*, edited by John Berkman and Michael Cartwright, 603–22. Durham, NC: Duke University Press, 2001.

———. *A Cross-Shattered Church: Reclaiming the Theological Heart of Preaching*. Grand Rapids: Brazos, 2009.

Hays, Richard B. *The Moral Vision of the New Testament: Community, Cross, New Creation; A Contemporary Introduction to New Testament Ethics*. New York: HarperSanFrancisco, 1996.

Heermann, Johann. "O God, My Faithful God." Translated by Catherine Winkworth. In *Trinity Hymnal*, rev. ed., 602. Suwanee, GA: Great Commission, 1990.

Hekman, Randall J. *Justice for the Unborn: Why We Have "Legal" Abortion and How We Can Stop It*. Ann Arbor, MI: Servant, 1984.

Hiebert, Paul G. *Transforming Worldviews: An Anthropological Understanding of How People Change*. Grand Rapids: Baker Academic, 2008.

Hollinger, Dennis P. *The Meaning of Sex: Christian Ethics and the Moral Life*. Grand Rapids: Baker Academic, 2009.

Holmes, Michael W., ed. *The Apostolic Fathers in English*. 3rd ed. Translated by Michael W. Holmes. Grand Rapids: Baker Academic, 2006.

Jacobsen, David Schnasa. "*Schola Prophetarum*: Prophetic Preaching Toward a Public, Prophetic Church." *Homiletic* 34, no. 1 (2009): 12–21.

James, P. D. *The Children of Men*. New York: Knopf, 1992.

Jelen, Ted G. "The Clergy and Abortion." *Review of Religious Research* 34 (1992): 132–51.

Jellinek, Michael S., et al. "Managed Health Care and Child Mental Health Services: Where Is Horton to Hear the Who's?" *Current Pediatric Reviews* 1 (2005): 31–37.

John Paul II. *The Gospel of Life (Evangelium Vitae): On the Value and Inviolability of Human Life*. Washington, DC: United States Catholic Conference, 1995.

Johnson, Luke Timothy. *The Gospel of Luke*. Sacra Pagina 3. Collegeville, MN: Liturgical, 1991.

Johnston, Robert K. *Reel Spirituality: Theology and Film in Dialogue*. 2nd ed. Engaging Culture. Grand Rapids: Baker Academic, 2006.

Jones, David Albert. *The Soul of the Embryo: An Inquiry into the Status of the Human Embryo in the Christian Tradition*. London: Continuum, 2004.

Jones, R. K., et al. "Abortion in the United States: Incidence and Access to Services, 2005." *Perspectives on Sexual and Reproductive Health* 40 (2008): 6–16.

Kachun, Mitch. *Festivals of Freedom: Memory and Meaning in African American Emancipation Celebrations, 1808–1915*. Amherst: University of Massachusetts Press, 2003.

Kaiser, Walter C., Jr. *What Does the Lord Require?: A Guide for Preaching and Teaching Biblical Ethics*. Grand Rapids: Baker Academic, 2009.

Keller, Tim. "Religion-less Spirituality." *Leadership*, Fall 1999, 25–26.

Keller, Timothy. *Counterfeit Gods: The Empty Promises of Money, Sex, and Power, and the Only Hope that Matters*. New York: Dutton, 2009.

———. *The Reason for God: Belief in an Age of Skepticism*. New York: Dutton, 2008.

Keller, Timothy J. *Ministries of Mercy: The Call of the Jericho Road*. 2nd ed. Phillipsburg, NJ: P & R, 1997.

———. "Preaching the Gospel in a Post-Modern World." Unpublished DMin syllabus, Reformed Theological Seminary, 2002.

Kline, Meredith G. "*Lex Talionis* and the Human Fetus." *Journal of the Evangelical Theological Society* 20 (1977): 193–201.

Klusendorf, Scott. *The Case for Life: Equipping Christians to Engage the Culture*. Wheaton, IL: Crossway, 2009.

———. "My Challenge to Christian Leaders: Preach and Equip." No pages. Online: http://lti-blog.blogspot.com/2007/09/my-challenge-to-christian-leaders.html.

Koloze, Jeff. "Abortion and Rap Music: A Literary Study of the Lyrics of Representative Rap Songs." In *Life and Learning XIII, Proceedings from the 13th Annual Conference of the University Faculty for Life, 2003*, 103–18. Washington, DC: University Faculty for Life, 2004.

Kreeft, Peter. *Three Approaches to Abortion: A Thoughtful and Compassionate Guide to Today's Most Controversial Issue*. San Francisco: Ignatius, 2002.

Kristof, Nicholas D. "Evangelicals a Liberal Can Love." No pages. Online: http://www.nytimes.com/2008/02/03/opinion/03kristof.html.

Kyle, Renee. "'You Care for Everybody': Cameron's Ethics of Care." In *House and Philosophy: Everybody Lies*, edited by Henry Jacoby, 125–36. Blackwell Philosophy and Pop Culture. Hoboken, NJ: Wiley, 2009.

Lake of Fire. DVD. Directed by Tony Kaye. Velocity/Thinkfilm, 2008.

Lewis, C. S. *The Screwtape Letters; also includes "Screwtape Proposes a Toast."* New York: HarperCollins, 2000.

Lim, Paul Chang-Ha. "*The Reformed Pastor* by Richard Baxter (1615–1691)." In *The Devoted Life: An Invitation to the Puritan Classics*, edited by Kelly M. Kapic and Randall C. Gleason, 152–66. Downers Grove, IL: InterVarsity, 2004.

Lloyd-Jones, D. Martyn. *Preaching and Preachers*. Grand Rapids: Zondervan, 1971.

Lovelace, Richard F. *Dynamics of Spiritual Life: An Evangelical Theology of Renewal.* Downers Grove, IL: Inter-Varsity, 1979.

Luther, Martin. "Disputation of Doctor Martin Luther on the Power and Efficacy of Indulgences." No pages. Online: http://www.iclnet.org/pub/resources/text/wittenberg/luther/web/ninetyfive.html.

———. *Luther's Works.* 4 vols. Edited by Jaroslav Pelikan. St. Louis: Concordia, 1958.

———. *What Luther Says: An Anthology.* Compiled by Ewald M. Plass. St. Louis: Concordia, 1959.

MacNair, Rachel, et al., eds. *Prolife Feminism: Yesterday and Today.* New York: Sulzburger & Graham, 1995.

Mannion, Michael T. *Abortion and Healing: A Cry to be Whole.* Kansas City, MO: Sheed & Ward, 1986.

Mansfield, Caroline, et al. "Termination rates after prenatal diagnosis of Down syndrome, spina bifida, anencephaly, and Turner and Klinefelter syndromes: a systematic literature review." *Prenatal Diagnosis* 19 (1999): 808–12.

Markos, Louis. *Apologetics for the 21st Century.* Wheaton, IL: Crossway, 2010.

Marshall, I. Howard. *The Gospel of Luke: A Commentary on the Greek Text.* New International Greek Testament Commentary. Grand Rapids: Eerdmans, 1978.

Mathewes-Green, Frederica. *Real Choices: Listen to Women; Looking for Alternatives to Abortion.* Ben Lomond, CA: Conciliar, 1997.

McClure, John S. *The Roundtable Pulpit: Where Leadership and Preaching Meet.* Nashville: Abingdon, 1995.

McComiskey, Thomas Edward. *The Minor Prophets: An Exegetical and Expository Commentary.* Vol. 1. Grand Rapids: Baker, 1992.

McLuhan, Marshall. "Private Individual vs. Global Village." In *Abortion and Social Justice*, edited by Thomas W. Hilgers and Dennis J. Horan, 245–48. New York: Sheed & Ward, 1972.

McLuhan, Marshall, and Eric McLuhan. *Laws of Media: The New Science.* Toronto: University of Toronto Press, 1988.

McMickle, Marvin A. *Where Have All the Prophets Gone?: Reclaiming Prophetic Preaching in America.* Cleveland: Pilgrim, 2006.

Melton, Gordon. *The Churches Speak On Abortion: Official Statements from Religious Bodies and Ecumenical Organizations.* Detroit: Gale Research, 1989.

Metzger, Bruce M. Foreword to *Abortion and the Early Church: Christian, Jewish and Pagan Attitudes in the Greco-Roman World*, by Michael J. Gorman, 9. Downers Grove, IL: InterVarsity, 1982.

Milavec, Aaron. *The Didache: Faith, Hope, and Life of the Earliest Christian Communities, 50–70 C.E.* New York: Newman, 2003.

Molinaro, Matie, et al., eds. *Letters of Marshall McLuhan.* Toronto: Oxford University Press, 1987.

Moore, Keith L., and T. V. N. Persaud. *The Developing Human: Clinically Oriented Embryology.* 6th ed. Philadelphia: Saunders, 1998.

Moore, Russell D. *Adopted for Life: The Priority of Adoption for Christian Families and Churches.* Wheaton, IL: Crossway, 2009.

Mother Teresa. "Whatever You Did unto One of the Least, You Did unto Me." In *The Right Choice: Pro-Life Sermons from . . .*, edited by Paul T. Stallsworth, 101–109. Nashville: Abingdon, 1997.

Motyer, Alec. *Look to the Rock: An Old Testament Background to Our Understanding of Christ*. Grand Rapids: Kregel, 2004.
Motyer, J. A. *The Day of the Lion: The Message of Amos*. The Bible Speaks Today. Downers Grove, IL: InterVarsity, 1974.
Mrozek, Andrea. "Canada's missing daughters." No pages. Online: http://www.canada.com/nationalpost/news/issuesideas/story.html?id=9faa3351-3db1-40d7-9e40-ccd59f4d3838.
Nathanson, Bernard N. *The Hand of God: A Journey from Death to Life by the Abortion Doctor Who Changed His Mind*. Washington, DC: Regnery, 1996.
Nathanson, Bernard N., and Richard N. Ostling. *Aborting America*. Garden City, NY: Doubleday, 1979.
National Abortion Federation. "Abortion Coverage by Region." No pages. Online: http://www.prochoice.org/canada/regional.html.
Neihart, Ben. "DGrassi Is tha Best Teen TV N da WRLD!" No pages. Online: http://www.nytimes.com/2005/03/20/magazine/20DEGRASSI.htm.
Neufeld, Gordon, and Gabor Maté. *Hold on to Your Kids: Why Parents Need to Matter More Than Peers*. New York: Ballantine, 2005.
Niederwimmer, Kurt. *The Didache: A Commentary*. Translated by Linda M. Maloney. Edited by Harold W. Attridge. Hermeneia. Minneapolis: Fortress, 1998.
O'Rahilly, Ronan, and Fabiola Müller. *Human Embryology and Teratology*. 3rd ed. New York: Wiley-Lass, 2001.
Olasky, Marvin. *Abortion Rites: A Social History of Abortion in America*. Wheaton, IL: Crossway, 1992.
Olsen, Ted. "More Important Than Christmas?: Why pro-life Protestants don't say much about the Annunciation—or the unborn Jesus." No pages. Online: http://www.christianitytoday.com/ct/2010/marchweb-only/22-41.0.html.
Ortlund, Dane C. "Christocentrism: An Asymmetrical Trinitarianism?" *Themelios* 34 (2009): 309–21.
Pahl, Michael W. "The 'Gospel' and the 'Word': Exploring Some Early Christian Patterns." *Journal for the Study of the New Testament* 29 (2006): 211–27.
Paul, Shalom M. *Amos*. Edited by Frank Moore Cross. Hermeneia. Minneapolis: Fortress, 1991.
Pavone, Frank A. "29 Reasons why pastors avoid taking a pro-life stand." No pages. Online: http://www.facebook.com/topic.php?uid=104966556423&topic=15275.
———. "Preaching to Children About Abortion." *Homiletic & Pastoral Review* (January 1996): 57–60. Online: http://www.catholiceducation.org/articles/abortion/ab0019.html.
———. "Talking Abortion." *Crisis* 15, no. 5 (1997): 14–17. Online: http://www.catholiceducation.org/articles/abortion/ab0001.html.
Philo. *On the Decalogue. On the Special Laws, Books 1–3*. Vol. 7. Translated by F. H. Colson. Loeb Classical Library 320. Cambridge: Harvard University Press; London: Heinemann, 1937.
Pierson, Anne, and Carol Risser. *52 Simple Things You Can Do To Be Pro-Life*. Minneapolis: Bethany House, 1990.
Piper, John. *Brothers, We Are Not Professionals: A Plea to Pastors for Radical Ministry*. Nashville: Broadman & Holman, 2002.
———. "How is trying to stop abortion different from physically intervening to stop child abuse?" No pages. Online: http://www.desiringgod.org/ResourceLibrary/

AskPastorJohn/ByTopic/47/3504_How_is_trying_to_stop_abortion_different_from_physically_intervening_to_stop_child_abuse/.
———. "When Is Abortion Racism?" No pages. Online: http://www.desiringgod.org/ResourceLibrary/Sermons/ByDate/2007/1951_When_Is_Abortion_Racism.
Piper, John, and Justin Taylor, eds. *Sex and the Supremacy of Christ*. Wheaton, IL: Crossway, 2005.
Pope, Charles. "Pondering Abortion in the African American Community." No pages. Online: http://blog.adw.org/2011/02/primer-on-black-abortions/.
Powlison, David. *Healing After Abortion: God's Mercy Is for You*. Greensboro, NC: New Growth, 2008.
———. "Idols of the Heart and 'Vanity Fair.'" *Journal of Biblical Counseling* 13, no. 2 (1995): 35–50.
———. *Seeing with New Eyes: Counseling and the Human Condition Through the Lens of Scripture*. Phillipsburg, NJ: P & R, 2003.
ProWomanProLife. "The Story." No pages. Online: http://www.prowomanprolife.org/the-story/.
Riols, Noreen. *My Unknown Child: A Personal Story of Abortion*. London: Hodder & Stoughton, 1995.
Robinson, Haddon W. *Biblical Preaching: The Development and Delivery of Expository Messages*. 2nd ed. Grand Rapids: Baker Academic, 2001.
Ryken, Philip G. *The Message of Salvation: By God's Grace, for God's Glory*. The Bible Speaks Today. Downers Grove, IL: InterVarsity, 2002.
Saward, John. *Redeemer in the Womb: Jesus Living in Mary*. San Francisco: Ignatius, 1993.
Schlossberg, Terry, and Elizabeth Achtemeier. *Not My Own: Abortion and the Marks of the Church*. Grand Rapids: Eerdmans, 1995.
Schultze, Quentin J. *Habits of the High-Tech Heart: Living Virtuously in the Information Age*. Grand Rapids: Baker Academic, 2002.
Schwarz, Benjamin. "Mad About Mad Men." No pages. Online: http://www.theatlantic.com/magazine/archive/2009/11/mad-about-i-mad-men-i/7709/.
Schwarz, Stephen. *The Moral Question of Abortion*. Chicago: Loyola University Press, 1990.
Selby, Terry L., and Marc Bockmon. *The Mourning After: Help for the Postabortion Syndrome*. Grand Rapids: Baker, 1990.
Sider, Ronald J. *The Scandal of Evangelical Politics: Why Are Christians Missing the Chance to Really Change the World?* Grand Rapids: Baker, 2008.
Sire, James W. *Naming the Elephant: Worldview as a Concept*. Downers Grove, IL: InterVarsity, 2004.
Sisk, Ronald D. *Preaching Ethically: Being True to the Gospel, Your Congregation, and Yourself*. Herndon, VA: Alban Institute, 2007.
Smith, Christine M. *Preaching as Weeping, Confession, and Resistance: Radical Responses to Radical Evil*. Louisville: Westminster, 1992.
Smith, Gary V. *The Prophets as Preachers: An Introduction to the Hebrew Prophets*. Nashville: Broadman & Holman, 1994.
Smith, Ralph L. *Micah-Malachi*. Word Biblical Commentary 32. Waco, TX: Word, 1984.
Snodgrass, Klyne. *Ephesians*. NIV Application Commentary. Grand Rapids: Zondervan, 1996.

Spaemann, Robert. *Persons: The Difference between 'Someone' and 'Something.'* Translated by Oliver O'Donovan. Oxford Studies in Theological Ethics. Oxford: Oxford University Press, 2006.

Sproul, R. C. *Abortion: A Rational Look at An Emotional Issue*. 2nd ed. Orlando: Reformation Trust, 2010.

Spurgeon, C. H. *Lectures to My Students*. London: Marshall, 1954.

Statistics Canada. "Induced Abortion Statistics, 2005." Online: http://www.statcan.gc.ca/pub/82-223-x/82-223-x2008000-eng.pdf.

Stewart, James S. *Heralds of God: A Practical Book on Preaching*. Vancouver: Regent College Publishing, 2001.

Stott, John R. W. *The Preacher's Portrait: Some New Testament Word Studies*. Grand Rapids: Eerdmans, 1961.

Strom, Bill. "What Is a Christian Worldview?" In *Christian Worldview and the Academic Disciplines: Crossing the Academy*, edited by Deane E. D. Downey and Stanley E. Porter, 13–34. McMaster Divinity College Press General Series 1. Eugene, OR: Pickwick, 2009.

Taylor, Justin. "'Abortion Is about God': Piper's Passionate, Prophetic Pro-Life Preaching." In *For the Fame of God's Name: Essays in Honor of John Piper*, edited by Sam Storms and Justin Taylor, 328–50. Wheaton, IL: Crossway, 2010.

Tertullian. *Apology. De Spectaculis*. Translated by T. R. Glover. Loeb Classical Library 250. Cambridge: Harvard University Press; London: Heinemann, 1931.

Tickle, Phyllis. "What We Would Like You to Know: A Preface." In *Confessing Conscience: Churched Women on Abortion*, edited by Phyllis Tickle, 9–12. Nashville: Abingdon, 1990.

Tisdale, Lenora Tubbs. *Preaching as Local Theology and Folk Art*. Minneapolis: Fortress, 1997.

U. S. Census Bureau. "The 2010 Statistical Abstract: Family Planning, Abortions." No pages. Online: http://www.census.gov/compendia/statab/cats/births_deaths_marriages_divorces/family_planning_abortions.html.

Van Der Horst, P. W. "Pseudo-Phocylides: A New Translation and Introduction." In *The Old Testament Pseudepigrapha*. Vol. 2, edited by James H. Charlesworth, 565–82. Garden City, NY: Doubleday, 1985.

Volf, Miroslav. *Exclusion and Embrace: A Theological Exploration of Identity, Otherness, and Reconciliation*. Nashville: Abingdon, 1996.

Walsh, Brian J., and J. Richard Middleton. *The Transforming Vision: Shaping a Christian Worldview*. Downers Grove, IL: InterVarsity, 1984.

Waltke, Bruce K. *The Book of Proverbs: Chapters 15–31*. New International Commentary on the Old Testament. Grand Rapids: Eerdmans, 2005.

———. *Micah: An Introduction and Commentary*. Tyndale Old Testament Commentaries. Leicester, UK: Inter-Varsity, 1988.

———. "Old Testament Texts Bearing on Abortion." *Christianity Today*, November 8, 1968, 99–105.

———. "Reflections from the Old Testament on Abortion." *Journal of the Evangelical Theological Society* 19 (1976): 3–13.

Walton, Rus. *Biblical Solutions to Contemporary Problems: A Handbook*. Brentwood, TN: Wolgemuth & Hyatt, 1988.

Wannenwetsch, Bernd. "Angels with Broken Wings: What the Disabled Teach Us About Our Common Humanity." Lecture at Regent College, Vancouver, BC, July 20, 2009.

———, ed. *Who Am I?: Bonhoeffer's Theology through His Poetry*. London: T & T Clark, 2009.

White, Barbara J. "A Call to Moral Leadership." In *BioEngagement: Making a Christian Difference through Bioethics Today*, edited by Nigel M. de S. Cameron, Scott E. Daniels, and Barbara J. White, 181–85. Grand Rapids: Eerdmans, 2000.

Whitehead, John W., ed. *Arresting Abortion: Practical Ways to Save Unborn Children*. Rutherford Institute Report 4. Westchester, IL: Crossway, 1985.

Willke, J. C. *Abortion and Slavery: History Repeats*. Cincinnati: Hayes, 1984.

Wilson, Paul Scott. *The Four Pages of the Sermon: A Guide to Biblical Preaching*. Nashville: Abingdon, 1999.

———. *Imaginations of the Heart: New Understandings in Preaching*. Nashville: Abingdon, 1988.

Wolterstorff, Nicholas. *Justice: Rights and Wrongs*. Princeton: Princeton University Press, 2008.

Youngblood, Ronald F. *Exodus*. Chicago: Moody, 1983.

www.ingramcontent.com/pod-product-compliance
Lightning Source LLC
Chambersburg PA
CBHW051949160426
43198CB00013B/2376